Words Words WORDS

G.M. Lupo

Lupo Digital Services, LLC
Atlanta, GA

First edition (paperback).

ISBN: 978-0-9981595-1-5. Published by Lupo Digital Services, LLC, Atlanta, Georgia (www.lupo.net). Printed in the United States of America.

Acknowledgements

The author wishes to thank everyone who purchased one of the individual volumes and especially those who have read and provided feedback on stories or essays. Special thanks to Sigrid Economou and Melissa Mullaney for your support and encouragement.

Other Work by the Author

G. M. Lupo is the author of these works:

- Rebecca, Too
- Atlanta Stories: Fables of the New South
- Faces in the Crowd (Kindle/eBook)
- Killing Babies: Collected Essays (Kindle)
- The Cheese Toast Project (Kindle)
- Freedom and Consequence (Kindle)
- The Long-Timer Chronicles (Kindle)

For new stories in development visit the author's blog Raised by Wolves at http://gmlupo.com.

G. M. Lupo can be found on the web at http://lupo.com.

To contact the author or to be added to the mailing list for future releases, send an email to author@gmlupo.com.

A Writer's Manifesto

The most important weapon in a writer's arsenal is language; wield it with skill and precision.

The writing should always speak for itself; never explain; never apologize, but always be willing to edit for clarity.

Don't worry about telling the literal truth; be true to the characters, the story, and the artistic vision.

Never consider anything finished; always look for ways to be more concise without compromising the story.

Listen to the readers; their feedback will indicate if the desired message has been conveyed.

Stop writing just prior to the point a reader is most likely to stop reading.

Avoid profanity unless no other means of expression will convey the point; if the writing is compelling, no one will miss it.

Understand that it usually takes many revisions to make the writing seem spontaneous.

Be aware that there is no such thing as realism in literature; all language is metaphorical, even when stating the facts.

Always keep in mind that it is not the writer who determines if the work is profound or relevant.

Realize that no amount of literary skill can save a piece if the writer doesn't know what needs to be said.

When all other plot points fail, kill the mother.

Faces in the Crowd

The volume of poetry these were taken from was published as an ebook in 2019. Most of these poems were written between high school and my undergraduate years in college. Earlier versions were published on my blog, and on my Internet homepage.

The most recent poem I have written is "Darwin's Progeny" during the mid-nineties.

The original version of "In Tribute" was written for and appeared in the 1981 edition of the William H. Russell High School yearbook, The Pointer, and represents my first published work.

"In a Restaurant", "Little League", and "Window Shopping" appeared in issues of The GSU Review between 1984 and 1986.

"Brain Cancer" was written in the margins of a page of notes I was taking in class my senior year of high school and remains the best statement about myself that I have ever written.

Brain Cancer

Who I am
I do not know,
for darkness lies
a blanket in my mind,
a shroud upon
the window to my soul.
My face unknown,
my name not called
and yet a sense of worth
escapes me not.

I am a man,
unknown to time,
existing only in my mind,
and with this thought
I am as naught,
but just a prisoner,
held in life,
consumed by death,
pitiless, yet pitied
by my peers,
unknown to me,
but not to he
who I should be.

Compensation

Some soft-muscled kid,
sand kicked in his face,
grows up to write movies
where the tough guys lose.
Late night, soft-white GE light
shines down on his battle-page,
him cast as the victor,
shattering the myth
that girls only like the jocks.
Red blood ink spills from
the pen, his sword
as he lops off the head
of some bar-belled body built,
clean-cut Adonis.
His night is productive,
as he wins another round,
another scene.
The morning finds him
slumped over his work,
the green gleam
on his phone machine
calling him to arms again.

Late Night Poet

The staccato rhythm of the
broken typewriter echoes
throughout the room
and disappears outside.
Increasing the size of the
paper heap in the trashcan,
a young man finds himself
no closer to solving earthly
mysteries than this time
last year.

Giving up on silence,
glaring at the noisy cat
which meowed its way
into the room a while ago,
he again hears words inside
his near-frustrated mind.
Somehow, though,
paper just doesn't seem
to capture
the effect.

Artistry

A chilling wind
blows by outside.
Scattered gusts enter
the window of
the small studio,
fighting back the
faint warmth
of an overworked
radiant heater.
A young man stands
before his easel
reproducing on canvas
the gaunt, hollow-eyed,
skeletal figures
which attack him
in his dreams.
Five floors below
the people of the city
are just leaving their jobs,
headed home from
another day of
phone calls, and meetings,
and endless paperwork.
He doesn't notice.
The blues and blacks
on the canvass
consume him.

A mouthful of coffee
helps him
regain his perspective.
One step back, then
a swirl of the brush
brings out maroon
figures dancing across
the bleak landscape,
then a streak of white
for contrast.
Another pause,
he tries to see it
like the viewer might.
He scratches his nose,
leaving a red mark,
which matches
the blue one
he made an hour ago.
As he works
into the night,
the darkness
on the canvass
begins to take shape,
becoming both
his masterpiece and
his mirror.

Artistry

The Nomad

His footsteps echo
in the corridors
of darkened alleyways
sparked with streetlamps.
He searches garbage cans
for succulent morsels
of 7:30 dinners
now forgotten.
He passes by
and I turn away
living within
the sunken dream
of another man's reality.

Window Shopping

An old man looked
through the jewelry
store window
at a young couple pricing
engagement rings.
Their faces glowed
with anticipation
of their coming life.
The old man
turned away with
memories rolling
down his cheeks
and made his way
on down the road.

Late Night Specters

Barefoot man in the restaurant,
his voice knows the names
of all who pass his way.
Older man than me,
his future is not secure,
but no one's ever is.
Shoeless friend, to all but me
knows more of life
than I could ever hope to,
not because he's lived it better,
but because the two seem to have
an understanding between them.

Big Fish, Little Fish

Through the streets you glide.
Cool white teeth gleam as you prey
on lonely pedestrians, never taking
their offered tokens
of Lincoln, Jackson, or VISA.
One quick knife click,
razor sharp slash, then off to find the next.
Each time, you corner in an alley
some grey-haired man or woman
or someone younger. It never matters.
Just the pleas, and the sobs
then the silence, better than sex.
They never see you coming
with your sleek, swift blade that strikes
then vanishes, leaving behind
your trail of blood, a feeding frenzy
for the press, who almost love you,
calling you "the Shark" and you feed on this
growing stronger, bolder. Until that night
you come upon the boy
walking swiftly ahead of you.
You follow into an alley, and strike.
The first slash cuts deeply, but he is quick;
tumbles out of your way and like
a slow-motion replay comes back up,
one arm extended and you laugh.
In the darkness of the alley you cannot see
the object in his hand nor hear the click.
But as you circle you hear the blast,
and feel yourself tossed back into a pile
of trash bags. With your final breath, you realize.
You're not the big fish anymore.

Darwin's Progeny

You too are smart, O worthy cousins.
With curious, intelligent eyes
you watch us tear the house down.
How you must wonder why,
must lament that, for a tiny quirk
in a microscopic strand
you could be the masters of the world.
Would we watch you
with the same concerns?

Undecided

I've had my lights
knocked out before.
Still the light shines from above.
I've heard the thunder,
felt the rain,
but blue skies always came again.
I've felt the madness,
known the fear,
to be alone in droves of friends.
I've been alone.
I may still be.
Who knows?

The Cat on my Wall

A cat sat on my garden wall.
Its eyes burned like a fire.
I watched it nearly half an hour,
Then off it quickly ran.

I sat awhile, with curtain drawn,
My life upon that wall.
The cat was gone, still I stayed on.
It's strange how life seems planned.

When she grew up, she could not be
in cramped places, like her mother's
walk-in closet, or the space between
her aunt's house and the garage.
Sometimes, in a theater, in that moment
of darkness before the movie flickered on,
she'd feel her throat tighten, and sweat begin
on her forehead, and she'd think back
to the time when she didn't know how long
the lights would be out.

Then there were times when she went back,
felt the chill of the dirt beneath her,
heard the digging which seemed to come
from all around. She remembered how she cried,
though her parents could not come to her.
That was when she learned
there is no Superman.

When she grew up, she was popular,
top of her class and everyone's best friend.
She seemed to know where the
best parties were held, and where
the most people would be.
In church, hers was the sweetest voice in the choir
but as she listened to the preacher,
who spoke of heaven and the rewards
that awaited all true Christians, she would laugh,
for there was nothing he could tell her.

> She already knew how it felt
> to be in the ground,
> then lifted up.

The Girl in the Well

Faces

We all have places
we would be,
if but the choice were ours.
We all have lives
we would have lived,
if born in other days.
Perhaps tomorrow
we shall find
a way to change our fates,
but for today
we shall remain
just faces in the crowd.

If

If I am just an actor
And all the world a stage
Should I be content to know
The lines upon the page?
And if I'm just an animal
Held within a cage
Would I be shot down if I
Someday break out in rage?
Would the world just stop and stare
If I weren't like the rest;
If I decide someday that I refuse
To take the test?
And if each man's an island
Dependent on himself
Would he object if he could not
Go on to greater wealth?
So it seems philosophy
Is not the thing for me.
But I'll go on and be myself
For no one else I'll be.

No beach to play on
Since you are gone
No field to run in
I'm all alone
No holding hands
While the movie is on
No room for heroes
Now that we're grown

No land of make believe
No Mouseketeers
No Sesame lyrics
To plague our ears
No snow at Christmas
Santa has gone
No room for heroes
Now that we've grown

No flowers for you
No bells to chime
No schoolboy love notes
I've got no time
No more of your life
And as for my own
No room for heroes
Now we have grown

No room for heroes

No beach to walk on
No time to share
No need to be happy
I no longer care
No time for memories
I'm all alone
No room for heroes
Now we are grown

Graduation Night

I feel somehow that I have
lived this scene before,
taken these measured steps toward
the final event of my youth.
I don't know when,
but once, I'm sure I saw the faces,
heard the speeches,
heard my name
called with the rest.

> I see them now, together,
> gold-robed figures walking straight,
> heads held high.
> I hear the murmurs of the crowd
> as they beckon for the end.
> No one realizes that the end
> is a long way off
> and that this is
> only a beginning.

Our teachers say, when this is over,
we will go our separate ways,
and forget the memories of our past
and of this night.
Still, though, I feel
that somewhere, someday, someway,
we will again be together as a group.

In Tribute

To the William H. Russell High School Graduating Class of 1981

Yesterday's children, obscured from sight,
Burst up through time and into the light.
Stand amongst honor and take your bow.
Yesterday's children have all grown up now.
Though years you've labored, toiled and strained,
Year after year you faced it again.
So now you are ready, rise up and cheer,
For now you've reached your final year.
Gone is your childhood, your happiest days.
You're now prepared for life's odd ways.
So stand and brave your finest hour,
Receive your diploma and take your flower.
Remember not your trials and tumults,
Look forward now, you are now young adults.

Speakeasy

Sit down my friends
and drink your cares away
as though there's nothing
to concern you.
Sit down my friends
and never mind
about the clock.
We all have problems,
that is true, but, for tonight
just let them slip away
and have a drink on me.
We're only here for
such a short time. So
my friends, please
sit down.

Carnation

The sound of music reaches my ears.
Music from a time gone by
which now to most is just a shadow.
Ages fly by quickly,
giving no one time to question why.
I know not why myself nor do I care.
Just fetch me my top hat,
and my gold-handled walking stick
and yes, we mustn't forget
my boutonniere.
I must look my best; for tonight
I have a date with destiny.

Little League

The small figure stands,
clinching the bat,
waiting for the final pitch.

His chest heaves once,
and he glances toward the stands
where his mother used to sit.

He sees the quick, white spot
moving toward him, swings,
and knocks it out of the park.

In a Restaurant

The cook smiles
at an entering guest,
taking short orders
all the while.
Two policemen sit,
enjoying their coffee,
dismissing thoughts
of outside incidents.
A young man orders
a burger to go.
He'll soon hitch a ride
to another town.
I sit back and watch
as the rain outside
makes rings
in tiny pools of water.

The sun goes down,
worlds darken.
Deep within
another tainted dream
I wander,
alone, with only
myself as companion.
Dusty hallways
fade in light.
Eerie screams
pierce tortured silence,
leaving only scattered bits
of broken dreams;
just memories.

Dreams and Less

Killing Babies

These essays are mostly from the collection of the same name published in 2016. *In the Bleak Midwinter* and *Icons*, were released on my blog in 2018, and not originally published with this collection. *War of Words* and *What Nature Intended* contain portions of several essays originally published as separate works.

A Form of Autobiography

The common advice to writers just starting out is to write what one knows, and often, this is good advice. What better starting point can an individual have than his or her own experiences and memories? To this end, many writers, such as Ernest Hemingway and Jack London led adventurous lives — Hemingway drove an ambulance during the Spanish Civil War, and London based his earliest stories on adventures he had during the Klondike Gold Rush. Other writers, such as Edgar Allen Poe and H. P. Lovecraft looked inward for the inspiration underlying their dark tales, drawing upon their fears and anxieties to craft their art.

At some point, a writer must face the fact that everything he or she writes is autobiographical on some level. The trick is making it seem like it isn't; otherwise, one is dealing with memoirs or journalism. Hemingway worked as a correspondent during World War II and his fictional work reflected the concise language of the reporter. While his novels benefited from a journalistic economy of words, his tales are just as fanciful as anything dreamed up by Poe. Still there is a level of authenticity to their work which no doubt came from knowing the people and circumstances chronicled.

In my own writing, I sometimes have trouble crafting male characters because they often come out sounding like me. The ironic thing is that many times the female characters sound like me, too, but because of the gender differences, no one pays attention. Rather than populating my work with actual people I know, I sometimes build composites of characters, a certain quirk from one person, a physical description from someone I've seen on television, a profession I may have read about. I once cast the supervisor from a job I had in college as the manager in an office patterned after a place I worked just after high school. My short story, *The Miracle of the Magic Dollar*, is largely based on an actual incident which happened in an office where I was working, though embellished for humorous effect.

Writers are often asked if characters are based on people they actually know, and in my case, they're usually based on people I'd like to know, with a sprinkling of characteristics of "real" people. Sometimes I'm inspired by a photo, a phrase, a quick glimpse of someone I see on the street, a snatch of dialogue heard on the train. My brain sometimes seems like an overstuffed trunk, brimming with ideas, lines, imagined scenes, all waiting for someplace to work. I carried the opening scene of my novel Crazy Like the Foxes around in my head for over twenty years, first conceiving it in the late-80s when I was in college and finally committing it to paper in 2006, when I sat down to write the novel on which Foxes is based.

I sometimes find other circumstances creeping into my work. When I was a child, a girl I knew died from leukemia, and that has found its way into my writing from time to time. Auto accidents also figure prominently in my work, having been in a few myself as well as losing a cousin to one around the time I was in college. I sometimes find myself developing ideas in my head for television shows I watch, and I still retain several treatments which have outlasted the shows for which they were conceived. Perhaps, someday, I'll commit these to paper in an altered context.

Inspiration comes from many sources, and writers must remain open to ideas regardless of the source. Past history and personal experiences can be excellent sources for material so long as one can record the truth of the experience without necessarily recounting the details of the incident to protect the privacy of others who were involved. Writers often have the luxury of distance and should always be willing to use whatever means to make the work as rich and meaningful as possible.

In the Bleak Midwinter

Nothing in his life became him like the leaving of it.
—Shakespeare, *Macbeth*

Without looking it up, how many people know John F. Kennedy's birthdate? Most people over a certain age can not only recall the date on which he died, but can relate, in great detail, where they were when they heard the news, and even those who weren't living at the time still know the date and circumstances. Numerous conspiracies surround the Kennedy assassination, including the rumor that JFK survived, and lived for many years afterward as an invalid. JFK looms largest in our memories not for what he did — in fact, for his day, he was a typical politician — but for what he might have done.

So, which is more important, that a person lived or that this person died? Dying isn't something unusual for biological entities. In fact, it's the one thing all living things have in common, that one day we shall die. We hear of people dying "before their times" but the moment of one's death is exactly one's time. People who are fortunate to live long, productive lives, are often celebrated instead of being mourned, though the loss is just as permanent as someone who dies without having lived up to his or her fullest potential. Everyone has heard of the "27 Club" of performers who tragically died at age twenty-seven, including Jimi Hendrix, Janis Joplin, Kurt Cobain, and Amy Winehouse. Some artists, such as Hendrix and Tupak Shakur, were more prolific after their deaths than before, having left behind a considerable body of work.

The Apostle Paul was a contemporary of and interacted with the Jerusalem Church run by Jesus's disciples, and since he was an adult while writing his epistles around 50 CE, he would have been alive during the events depicted in the Gospels. Despite this, he rarely talks about the life or teachings of Jesus, but of the resurrection of the Christ; "...if Christ has not been raised, our preaching is useless and so is your faith" (1 Corinthians 15:14, NIV). In fact, the path to salvation presented in 1 Corinthians 15, totally excludes following the teachings of Jesus: Christ died; was buried; rose from the dead. All followers need to do is believe that. It was nearly twenty years following the writings of Paul that Mark, acknowledged by most scholars as the first Gospel, depicts the life events of a man identified in the original Greek as Jesus. His actual name was most likely Yeshua or Jeshua, and this name has also come into English as Joshua, which is the name of the Biblical hero who led the conquest of Canaan, meaning there were likely lots of guys named Yeshua in Palestine at the time.

One of the debates in the early church was whether faith alone or faith with good deeds guaranteed salvation (James 2:14-26) and James seems to attach much importance to one's deeds. This debate was one of the issues that sparked the Protestant Reformation centuries later. Martin Luther declared that faith alone is the path to salvation, and many Christians today continue to hold this belief. To a lot of people, it doesn't matter that Jesus is quoted as saying, "Do unto others as you would have them do unto you", or "Love your neighbor as yourself", or "Turn the other cheek", just that he died, was resurrected, and they believe, which is the formula provided by Paul. Just as an early, unexpected death heightened the importance of JFK's presidency, Jesus's death seems to have inspired many stories and rumors among followers and detractors about what happened and what it all meant.

We need look no further than the rumors and iconography surrounding Elvis Presley to see similarities to the rumors and legends that evolved into the Gospels. Just like Jesus, Elvis was a charismatic individual, said to have survived or returned following his "death" and there are many elaborate theories about how and why Elvis faked his death and how and when he plans to reveal himself to his followers, all of which seem less and less likely as time goes on. Elvis Presley was born in 1935, and even if he is somehow still around, would be in his late-eighties today. It's highly unlikely he'd still be performing in Vegas even if he's alive.

There are still many people who were here when Elvis walked the Earth. We live in a media obsessed culture and have plenty of official reports to confirm Elvis's death, and only vague rumors of people who claim to have seen him alive after August of 1977. Still the rumors persist. People obviously saw Jesus crucified; it's stated that the women who surrounded him held vigil nearby and went to prepare his body after the Sabbath. The author of the Gospel of Matthew alludes to some of the rumors surrounding the disappearance of his body and mentions that the guards at the tomb were paid off by the high priest to say Jesus's followers stole his body (Matthew 28:11-15). Why would Matthew need to mention that fact if there weren't rumors floating around about it?

Everything living will someday die, that's the cold hard fact. No one likes to think of that possibility, and everyone wants to believe that somehow, there's a way to avoid it. No one can definitively say what becomes of us when we die. For many, a "better" world is waiting; for others, we simply drift off into nothingness. We like to think that those who died early are somehow waiting somewhere for the perfect time to reveal it was all a hoax. Many people are certain Andy Kaufman is doing just that but given how much he liked to "play" the audience, he'd probably be amused at how many people believe he's still alive. Perhaps, rather than focusing on a person's death, it's more instructive to examine how that person lived, for better or worse, to gain lessons on how we can better conduct our affairs.

For the record, John F. Kennedy was born 29 May 1917. I admit, I had to look it up.

Shadow Selves

We all have secret sides to our personalities that we keep hidden from those around us — thoughts we never share, opinions we never state, fantasies we never reveal. Each individual carries around multiple perspectives inside his or her mind, a unique vision that no one else can imagine or share. Artists tap into this reservoir to bring their views of reality to light, and often, in creating fiction, shine a spotlight on the truth. Often the people we imagine ourselves to be are in stark contrast to the faces we present to the world.

Jack Henry Abbot was an incarcerated felon who gained fame in the early 80s when his writing was published with the assistance of Norman Mailer as the bestselling work, *In the Belly of the Beast*. Critics praised his writing for its raw and powerful depiction of prison life. The recognition led to his being released from incarceration, and not long afterward, he murdered a man in an altercation outside a restaurant, returning him to prison.

One might wonder how such a violent individual could craft words with such intensity. The reality is that Abbot was both a brilliant writer and a hardened criminal. The aspects of his character which made him a violent felon may also have fueled his more poetic side. The tragedy for him and especially the man he killed was that he was unable to reconcile both sides within himself and overcome the violence he had known inside prison. He eventually took his own life behind bars.

We've all heard stories about people who hid aspects of their characters, the church deacon who was secretly molesting children; the homeless person who was a covert multimillionaire; the shy store clerk who no one knew could sing like an angel. Writers who publish under assumed names are often nothing like the characters they create. For every story of someone whose hidden side was brought to light, there are hundreds of others who never reveal who else may be lurking inside their heads.

The question is, which one is real? Are we the faces we present to the world or the compendium of voices which issue forth from our subconscious minds? We've all had moments when our actions astound even us. Confronted with a situation, we can imagine the absolute worst way we could respond, then proceed to do just that without being able to explain why. The question of nature versus nurture also looms large in our experience.

Are we the people we imagine ourselves to be or have we been conditioned by the circumstances of our lives?

The Internet has given rise to a similar phenomenon, quiet, unassuming people becoming trolls and cyber bullies online. I once knew an individual who posted in a news group I frequented. In the group, where he posted under his actual name, he often took a superior and insulting tone toward those who disagreed with his opinions. Whenever I'd bring up his online endeavors in person, however, he'd become defensive and wouldn't talk about it. He probably viewed his online persona as detached from his "real life" without recognizing how much a part of his character it was.

The truth is, we are whoever we define ourselves to be. It's common to see artists behaving in a manner that seems outside society's norms, but in reality, we all have people we'd like to be if certain constraints were removed. How much time and effort do we invest in being who we think others want us to be instead of concentrating on who we'd rather be?

Killing Babies

As one develops as a writer, one becomes aware of the painful reality that not everything one writes, no matter how well-crafted or heartfelt, will see the light of day. In many cases, favorite phrases or passages must be sacrificed for the overall good of the piece, and sometimes entire chapters or works-in-progress will be shelved. Improving the quality of the writing doesn't make excising them any easier though. With characters, who have a tendency to take on lives of their own, it can be very difficult making the call to remove them. The editing process is, sometimes, akin to killing a well-loved child.

A writer has just crafted the perfect paragraph, one that beautifully sums up the character and situation, all the while being witty, insightful, and concise and try as one might, it can't be worked into the context of the story in progress. I once crafted this opening paragraph:

> Aaron Slaughter was appropriately named. He was born bad and grew up mean and never did a kind turn for anyone, from the moment the doctor slapped him on the ass to the day they strapped him into the electric chair and put eighteen hundred volts through him. I was there that day, and while I'm not normally the sort of person to watch another human being die, I made an exception in Aaron's case. See, I'm the man who put him there.

As happy as I am with the paragraph, I have never been able to create a coherent story around it.

What's worse than being unable to use good material is having to remove it after fitting it into a work. Editing is actually where the real work of writing begins. Few writers are able to set words onto paper exactly the way they will eventually be finalized. I tend to be an organic writer and once I get into a work, the words flow with no rhyme or reason. Editing is crucial to my process, because when I'm writing, my only concern is getting the thoughts into words. As the work grows, a pattern begins to emerge and I can start rearranging paragraphs, adding and deleting lines until the piece says what I want in the way I want it said. Along the way, lots of favorite lines and phrases get cast aside.

Removing material does not mean it's bad, just as rejection of a manuscript or play doesn't mean the writing is lousy. It simply means the material does not work with the piece as a whole. I wrote an entire section for my novel *The Long-Timers* in which the main character was brought before the McCarthy hearings in the 1950s, which did not make it into the finished work. When I reworked the novel into A *Tale of Two Sisters*, however, I found a place for the material again. Oftentimes, material that doesn't fit in one work, may be just what's lacking in another.

Writers learn to maintain journals or files of ideas and phrases which may someday make it into a piece of writing. Carrying around miniature computers in our pockets makes this task easier. I like to retain text files of everything I remove from a story or play, since I may find a use for it somewhere else, and with the advent of Cloud computing and advances in programs such as Acrobat, I'm now able to edit documents anywhere and preserve drafts of works in progress.

In some cases, I've taken bits and pieces of excised material to fill out or enhance a different work or borrowed scenes from one play to use in another. For my play *Another Mother*, I created a mother/daughter relationship, which didn't survive the rewrites, but which found new life when I began serializing a story about a secondary character from the play, and the original family dynamic of Alyssa Caine from the earliest drafts of Rebecca, Too, found new life in a later work when I applied it to a different character.

Still, cutting scenes or paragraphs from a work isn't easy. "They're my babies," a writer might say. "I can't kill them!" If one is to evolve as a writer, however, it's a skill one must master. At one time, a publisher would pair an author with an editor who would take on the harsh process of excising passages, but with independent authors publishing their own work, a professional editor is often a luxury one simply cannot afford. It becomes the writer's responsibility to make the necessary cuts. No one will be seriously harmed if a novel, story, or play is a few hundred words shorter than the author initially conceived it — not even the author. The goal is always to say what one means as succinctly as possible, even if it means killing a few babies.

Bad Credit

We hear a lot about identity theft, and credit agencies spend billions every year combating it and advising the public on how to guard their personal information. This is ironic, since it's the credit industry that's solely responsible for identity theft in the first place. The very information stolen and used to create bogus accounts is the information compiled by credit agencies. A person's Social Security number was never supposed to be used for identification. Banks and creditors are the ones who started using it as such and it's often through compromised credit records that this information falls into the hands of the wrong people.

The credit reporting agencies that keep track of all our information were created by financial institutions and answer exclusively to them. Even the credit monitoring agencies, which alert consumers when suspicious activity is detected are products of the financial industry in its attempts to deal with a problem it has caused by charging people more to monitor the information they're already monitoring.

The amount of information the credit industry has on an individual is mind-boggling. I recently applied for a loan and among the questions I had to answer to verify my identity was the address of an apartment where I was living in New York nearly thirty years ago. It occurred to me that they have a record of every car I've financed, every home I've purchased, every credit card I've used. Since they have access to public records, they also know what property is in my name and any time there's been any sort of legal action taken against me. Their file on me continues to grow. While my personal credit record is not supposed to be available to the general public the way property records are, we've seen many examples recently of such information falling into the wrong hands.

At one time, charging exorbitant interest on loans was called loan-sharking and was illegal in this country. Now, it's standard business practice among the credit card companies. When I got my first credit card in the early-80s, it was possible for consumers to write off credit card interest on their taxes. One of the enduring legacies of the Reagan administration was that this was abolished during his term of office. It was once the banks who determined one's credit-worthiness for mortgages and car loans, now all those functions have been ceded to the credit agencies and we're none the better for it. Financial institutions have always had a very cozy relationship with politicians much to the benefit of the industry.

In 2008, the financial industry was responsible for the worst economic meltdown since the 1920s by playing fast and loose with the funds entrusted to them by investors and consumers. Most of what they were doing was, at one time, outlawed or heavily regulated by the government, but these rules were watered down by corporate friendly politicians throughout the 90s and 00s, as was much of the antitrust legislation passed in the early-20th Century. This allowed banks and other financial institutions to become "too big to fail" which was the argument for the government bailing them out. Many parts of the world are still reeling from the effects. Yet, it is highly unlikely that anyone responsible will be held accountable, especially since a lot of them serve as economic advisers to Congress and the President.

Alongside our horribly broken political system and the wretched way we handle healthcare in the United States, the financial industry is another sector of our country much in need of regulation and reform. Unfortunately, our elected officials have demonstrated time and again that the people who pad their pockets get first priority and the consumers at the bottom are more or less on their own in dealing with the problem. The financial industry has repeatedly demonstrated that it must be regulated or else it goes to any length to cut corners for higher profits. Pay day lenders, toxic credit swaps, and subprime mortgages are just a few of the avenues that have been employed by the financial industry to dupe consumers and rack up high profits and the people who suffer most are often low-income consumers least able to defend themselves. The fact that the lending agencies can foreclose on someone's home, then sell the property at a profit shows that all the power is in their hands.

In the days of mill towns, workers were forced to deal with the "company store" which sank them so far into debt that their only choice was to work long hours for demeaning wages just to maintain payments. Under this system, there was no hope of ever getting ahead, and workers sometime spent their entire lives working for the company with nothing to show for their efforts. Unionization helped workers overcome these horrible conditions, but over time many unions became corrupt or were targeted by union busting politicians working on behalf of corporations seeking to lower their bottom line. Along the way, the middle-class lifestyle that was the bedrock of the "American dream" has slowly been eroded away, with workers now spending more hours at work for much lower wages and forced to take out loans or use credit cards with high interest rates. Again, politicians have colluded with the same greedy business interests they're supposed to protect the public from to bring about the situation we now face.

Ultimately, it's in the hands of consumers to correct this state of affairs, but that means becoming better informed and taking more of an interest in politics at the national and especially the local levels. It means investing time in knowing where our elected officials stand on certain issues and who's financing their campaigns. Most important, it means holding our representatives accountable for their decisions and actions. It's not enough to continually rubber stamp candidates who promise to lower our taxes while being vague on their full agendas. As with everything in life, it requires work and diligence to bring about change, but the rewards are certainly worth it.

War of Words

In his novel, *1984*, George Orwell presents readers with a society so repressive that even the mere thought of dissent is outlawed. Every citizen has a 24-hour monitoring device installed in his or her home, and even the English vernacular has been altered to filter out the language of rebellion.

Those engaged in the discussion over "political correctness" on college campuses and in political discourse may feel they've entered the Oceania of Orwell's narrative. Everyday conversations are scrutinized for hidden innuendo as even the most mundane of intentions are viewed with microscopic precision to ferret out the secret agenda lurking behind. In many offices throughout the US, for example, it's no longer possible for a male coworker to compliment the appearance or dress of his female counterparts without setting himself up for several sessions of sensitivity training at the very least, and the heightened level of aversion to antagonistic points of view on college campuses generates much fodder for late night comics and network pundits.

The notion of "correcting" one's thoughts, can also be exploited by unscrupulous governments, anxious to control their populations. If a governing entity can teach its people to sensor their own thoughts, to filter out any notion of disagreement, then the state doesn't need to police the population as rigorously. Throughout history, religion has served that purpose, training people to trust their subjective faith and obey those in authority rather than listening to objective facts, and in repressive regimes like the former Soviet Union, the state relied on endless sloganeering and the ever-present shadow of the secret police to instill fear and compliance into the minds of its citizens. In less restrictive societies, those in charge utilize subtler means to insure people don't get out of hand.

The fact that people coexist peacefully is as much dependent upon the tendency of individuals to avoid conflict than any conditioning on the part of the state. Politicians have realized that when people are reasonably content, they usually won't work against the system that fosters their contentment. In the US, the only thing deadlier to one's political career than being branded "a liberal", is to propose raising taxes.

Part of the problem with political correctness is that it functions outside the boundaries of jurisprudence, where a simple accusation is enough to irreparably tarnish a person's reputation. If someone is branded a racist or sexist, regardless of whether or not that person exhibits such tendencies, the person has almost no defense, and any attempt to dispute the charge is taken as further evidence of the person's guilt. Often, worse consequences result, particularly in an era of rampant Internet shaming, where those unhappy with someone's actions go on the attack at the flimsiest of provocations, exposing private details on an individual and launching threats and insults both aimed at the target and anyone who dares to defend the person. Jobs have been lost and people forced into hiding as a result of actions people on the Internet found offensive.

Despite the potential for abuse, in a diverse society, there is good reason to train people to be more sensitive to how their words affect others. Often, when one is raised in a homogeneous community that has had little contact with divergent points of view, one's speech and attitudes tend to reflect the biases of that group. When one moves from that to the broader world, these biases can become problematic when dealing with people who are the focus of such attitudes.

For instance, calling someone "gay" as an insult ignores the impact this attitude has on individuals who are gay or lesbian. Sometimes insulting words can become part of the vernacular of a given people, to "welsh" on a deal, for instance, or by using the term "ghetto" when discussing the inner city. Most people aren't even aware of the cultural biases inherent in their speech and often become defensive when someone takes offense at a description or turn of phrase.

For centuries, those attempting to manipulate the public conscience have understood that appealing to emotions or instincts is far more effective than appealing to intellect. The advertising industry makes a fortune each year manipulating the audience's emotions to sell everything from coffee and toothpaste, to candidates for all levels of public office. In the old South, those in power recognized that working class blacks and whites had more in common with one another than with the wealthy and greatly out-numbered elite and cultivated the myth of white supremacy to keep the races from establishing common ground. This did not change the status of poor whites — they were as oppressed and exploited as before — but it made them feel superior and that served the purpose of the ruling elite.

Today, we have an entire mass market industry dedicated to

keeping people ignorant, uninformed, and conditioned to follow pre-determined prompts to react, either by consuming certain products, voting for candidates with narrow ideologies, or expressing outrage in other, less potent forms, such as meaningless polls, petitions, or public demonstrations. It's ironic that a large portion of the people who fail to vote in elections instead spend their time and efforts creating Internet memes or signing online petitions, none of which have any demonstrable effect on the process while ignoring a guaranteed method of effecting change through the ballot box.

The corporate news media is of little assistance, on one hand telling us how important it is to vote, all the while dismissing candidates as unelectable due to lack of party allegiance, or by skewing elections with endless polls and analysis favoring a particular candidate. The modern mass media is, in fact, the fulfillment of Orwell's worst nightmare, as outlined in his work *Politics and the English Language*, making lies sound truthful, murder respectable, and giving an appearance of solidity to the wind.

In this environment, words become almost meaningless and knowledge becomes a commodity to be traded for political advantage. Everyone claims exclusive access to "the truth" and barters this knowledge in exchange for unceasing devotion to a cause or candidate. People feel marginalized and latch on to the person or group who best assigns blame for the cause of those feelings. The result is increasing polarization as each group fights to promote its version of the "real" story. This situation is nothing new.

Most "revealed" religions begin with an individual or group claiming some sort of "divine" inspiration, then offering to share it in exchange for followers. Make no mistake, all religions are political, and those that do the best job of adapting their message to the needs of the power elite are often the ones which become prominent in society regardless of how truthful they are. Christianity is a leading religion today solely because Rome chose it as the state religion in the fourth or fifth century. Rather than faith, it was a political decision that led to the religion we now know.

The Gnostics, who were the chief rivals to the emerging Christian church in the second and third centuries of the Christian era, believed humans were trapped in their earthly bodies, and it was only through specialized knowledge or gnosis that they could escape. Christian Gnostics believed that Jesus had supplied such knowledge through secret teachings to his closest followers. Jesus himself is quoted in the Gospels as saying that he speaks in parables to the masses and reveals the true meaning only to his inner circle of disciples (see Mark 4:10-12, Matthew 13:10-17, and Luke 8:10-12).

Many of the Gnostic texts which managed to survive are allegorical and couched in paradoxical language that would seem confusing to someone not familiar with how to read it. To the uneducated masses, the simple and adaptable message of the Christian church was much easier to understand than the complicated wordplay of the Gnostics. Those who were initiated into the mysteries felt no need to share their secret insights with an unreceptive audience.

Much of the writing of the Gnostics was dismissed as heretical by the early Church and destroyed after the Catholic church won the battle for primacy in the West, though remnants found their way into the Christian canon, notably in the Gospel of John and the Apocalypse or Revelation of John ("I am Alpha and Omega; the first and the last"). One might suggest that because the Catholic church survived and the Gnostics didn't, the Church's beliefs must have been right, but it's equally true to observe that it's easier for a given set of beliefs to survive with the force of an empire behind it. The fact that the rise of Christianity yielded three official churches, the Orthodox church in the East, the Catholic church in the West, and the many Protestant denominations following Martin Luther's Reformation, each with its own orthodoxy and interpretation of the Bible, demonstrates that there was not unanimous agreement on the truth, even after the Gnostics had been eliminated and their ideology driven underground.

In today's society, an increasingly marginalized population finds many avenues by which to vent their anger and frustration, some more appropriate than others. One such area is the English-only movement which seeks to establish English as the official language of the United States and to require all newcomers to learn English as part of their paths to citizenship. More extreme elements of this movement want to prohibit those whose first language isn't English from being able to speak another language in public. These notions totally ignore the reality that, South of our borders and in our commonwealth of Puerto Rico, Spanish is the predominant language, and North of us is a large province which speaks French. Canada is a bilingual nation and hasn't suffered by being thus. To combat the idea that we should adopt a single language as our official tongue, appealing to the altruism of those demanding this change is useless. In fact, one of the arguments is that they should not have to learn another language simply to accommodate newcomers.

Words have always been used to achieve political ends, whether through limiting the topics acceptable for discussion, or by dictating the terms under which discussions take place, and the more obscure the presentation, the less likely individuals are to become engaged. The result is a population that's alienated, marginalized, and disconnected to the functions of society. So far, our representatives, who greatly benefit from this state of affairs, have shown little inclination to change. It's time to turn the tide and demand more from those who are supposed to be protecting our interests. With a little ingenuity and resourcefulness, we can win this war of words.

Break the Chains

How far removed are we from segregation in this country? On the day I was born in Atlanta, it was not possible for blacks and whites to eat in the same restaurant. That changed a few months later, so segregation has been a reality within my lifetime. People of different races could not marry in most of the US. That changed a few years later between the years my brothers were born. While much of the stigma society imposed upon mixed marriages has lessened, there are still many people opposed to those of different races being together. Given that it's been more than forty years since the legal restrictions on mixed race marriage were removed without gaining full acceptance in society, one can assume those who supported legalization of same sex marriage still have a long road ahead of them and will most likely never win total acceptance from every segment of the population.

One lingering problem within the United States is the institutionalized racism that exists at every level of society. The conservative right in this country has done an excellent job of conditioning citizens to equate the terms, "welfare", "government assistance", and "low income" with minorities. While it is true that a significant number of minority individuals are on public assistance, it is an unfair assumption to equate most people of a given race or ethnicity with low income or so-called "ghetto" conditions. The problem is that the attitude of many liberals is not much better, believing that minorities need public assistance because they can't take care of themselves.

Rather than arguing over the need for such safety nets, perhaps the politicians would be better advised to concentrate on the factors that lead to people requiring public assistance than debating whether or not assistance is needed. People will always have hard times, which require them to seek assistance from some outside source. Ironically, many people who oppose government programs are the people who could benefit from them. On the other hand, wealthy individuals will gladly contribute to charities or church funds which benefit the same people they would deny food stamps or other government aid.

The term "welfare queen" has come to represent people milking public assistance while wearing expensive shoes and driving Cadillacs, but the term was originally used for a specific individual, a Chicago woman most commonly identified as Linda Taylor, whose crimes included, but were not limited to living high on the public dole. While the press in Chicago dubbed her the "Welfare Queen" and detailed her many frauds, it was candidate and future president Ronald Reagan who brought her to the attention of the larger public, thus politicizing her story. "Welfare queens" is now racist code for minorities, particularly blacks, but the actual individual who inspired the term frequently lied about her race, and on her death certificate and census documents is listed as white (see "The Welfare Queen", Slate, 19 December 2013, online).

White people, as a group, rarely acknowledge the problem of institutional racism, largely because we're responsible for creating and maintaining it, and we benefit from it. There are many aspects of life I take for granted, even though I grew up in a lower middle-class setting. In most cases, when the police pull me over for a traffic offense, I don't fear that the encounter could result in my death. In fact, my complaint with the police is often that they don't seem responsive enough when something happens. I would not hesitate to contact them and while sometimes wary, I rarely fear encounters with them. I'm aware that many minorities do not have the same experiences or attitude, often with good reason. I'm more concerned that some deranged individual — with a high statistical probability that person will be white — will open fire in some space I'm inhabiting than I fear an encounter with police.

I grew up in rather unique circumstances, namely, when I was around eight to ten years old, Atlanta experienced "white flight" when whites from the inner city moved to the suburbs of Cobb and Gwinnett in response to blacks moving into their neighborhoods. In a relatively short amount of time, I went from being in the majority in my school to being in the minority. By the time I was in seventh grade, I was one of only five or six whites in either class, and below that, there were only four or five whites in the entire school, two of whom were my brothers. While this gave me some insight into how it felt to stand out in a group of people, and to experience hostility directed at me for no other reason than how I look, it did not cause me to experience what it's like to be a minority twenty-four hours, seven days a week in the US. While blacks and whites can be equally racist on a personal level, it's usually the whites who have the power and privilege to institutionalize racism.

Large, well-funded organizations like the NAACP, do a reasonable job of going after corporations or government institutions which foster institutionalized racism though it can be difficult to spot or prove. When the focus shifts from institutional to individual racism, the problem is a little more difficult to diagnose and correct. It is important to confront racism whenever encountered, but simply branding this individual or stand-alone organization racist doesn't always accomplish anything constructive, and frequently leaves the target bitter and more entrenched in his or her racist attitudes. Individuals see little incentive to change when the organization to which they belong or the company where they work fosters the same attitude, though it is, often, through the efforts of individuals that corporate cultures evolve.

The US has a long way to go in addressing racial disparities, but we accomplish nothing by pretending the problem does not exist. Too much hostility is directed at too many people and far too much blood has been spilled for us to turn a blind eye to what's happening. Our leaders need to work on solutions rather than fanning the flames of racial hatred, as the current presidential administration has been doing. We should applaud the efforts of those who are attempting to initiate a dialogue, but more importantly, we need to participate in the conversation.

Atlanta Transitional

As an Atlanta native, I always find it interesting to read lists of places or activities which characterize denizens of the city, many of which I hardly recognize. Lenox Square Mall, for instance, is cited as the place Atlanta shops, but it wasn't until I was in high school or college and driving places on my own that I went there on a regular basis, and then it was largely to buy records. Growing up in West End and East Point, I frequented The Mall West End, Lakewood, and Greenbriar Malls, later Southlake, and, to a lesser extent, Shannon Mall.

The same is true of Buckhead, where I didn't hang out regularly before mid- to late-college. Virginia Avenue and Old National Highway were the party spots for me and my friends in high school. To the best of my knowledge, I have never been inside the Clermont Lounge. At the time I'd have been most likely to go, in college in the eighties, that part of Ponce was considered very dangerous, particularly for foot traffic.

I also cannot recall eating at the Mary Mac, even though I'm distantly related to the family of the former owner of it and despite the fact that I have been to the Krispy Kreme doughnuts across the street. Living south of town, it always required a special trip to get to that part of Atlanta, and there were lots of southern style eateries in between.

When I was born, John F. Kennedy was president; Carl Sanders was governor of Georgia and Ivan Allen, Jr. was mayor of Atlanta. The Atlanta Crackers was the main professional sports team in town. Within my lifetime, Atlanta acquired the Braves, the Falcons, and the Hawks; acquired then sold the Flames and Thrashers and has even tried out soccer a few times, Atlanta United being the most successful incarnation by far. Atlanta-Fulton County Stadium was built, then demolished, as was the Omni, and the Georgia Dome.

While not much of a sports fan, I followed the Braves as a child. Despite all their success in the nineties, in my youth the team had a reputation for being lovable losers. They had great individual players such as Hank Aaron, Dale Murphy, and Phil Niekro, but were rarely able to pull together enough wins as a team to make it to the post season. I attended games in the seventies where we were happy if they won that particular game, let alone the pennant. An entire generation of Atlanta fans has now grown up with the Braves as the powerhouse contenders they were throughout the nineties and are, no doubt, disappointed when they don't live up to that reputation.

Growing up in Atlanta, I learned to not get too attached to specific places because they might not be there next time I visited. The Atlanta that people who relocated here in the seventies remember was built over top of the Atlanta I knew as a young child. At one point, the Polaris restaurant, the blue dome at the top of the Hyatt Regency, was one of the tallest structures in the city; now, one must be downtown to see it. Whenever I was traveling South on Peachtree Street in high school or early college, I frequently used the Coke sign at the intersection of Ivy Street to navigate. Now, not only is the Coke sign no longer there, Ivy Street was renamed Peachtree Center Avenue in the nineties.

I attended Georgia State University from 1982 through 1987 and usually commuted by bus, as the south line of MARTA was under construction during that time. Before I graduated, Lakewood station opened and my bus, 72 Airport, was rerouted there. At the time, GSU was confined to the central campus downtown. We didn't have a football team, and the basketball program wasn't all that great. There were no dorms, and the now heralded law school was in its infancy. Since I graduated, the university has expanded throughout the city, has a football program and the campus downtown has added numerous buildings either through purchase or construction. Riding past it on MARTA, I'm still able to recognize most of the campus but there are many new buildings I don't recall from my time there. One example is the Rialto, which was a cheap movie theater that showed Kung Fu films when I was in college, and now the name is synonymous with a world-renowned performing arts center.

I moved to New York in 1989 and moved back to Atlanta in 1994, two years before the Olympics were held here. In those five years, in preparation for the Games, the city changed greatly. Streets were renamed, businesses closed, buildings were demolished and replaced by new ones. MARTA completed the line out to the airport and rerouted, renamed, or discontinued several bus lines I had used. Even though I visited during the holidays, I wasn't spending much time traveling around mapping out how the city was changing. By the time I got back and started looking for work, I hardly recognized the place. When I left, for instance, Rio Mall had just opened with much fanfare, and by the time I returned, it was already in decline and since then the building has been demolished. Once the Games were over, many of the sporting venues were packed up and moved elsewhere. People who knew me around that time found it amusing that I'd sometimes get lost navigating around town, mainly because of all the changes to a city that was already difficult to navigate in the first place.

I served as president of the Atlanta Junior Chamber of Commerce, or Jaycees, from May 1997 until April 1998 and in my plan for the upcoming year, I noted that one of the problems we faced in maintaining a community service organization in Atlanta was the transient nature of our population. Most members at that time had been in town less than five years and would not be here five years after. Most were unmarried, apartment dwellers or condo owners, with no solid connection to the community. Most were upwardly mobile professionals, who spent a lot of time at work and in their off time didn't want to manage projects, an activity which characterizes many Jaycee chapters.

When I joined, I heard the chapter referred to as Atlanta's largest dating service and found this to be an apt description in some respects. Our members were more interested in social outings which introduced them to places or activities where they could unwind, enjoy themselves, and meet new people. While we did have a contingency of members with roots in the community, and those who were interested in community service, this did not represent a large segment of the membership. A fair number of people attended a function, joined the chapter, and afterward we never saw them again, or they joined, became active, then were relocated by their employers to another town. Needless to say, membership turnover was always a problem.

Transition has always been a central part of Atlanta's story. Perhaps the most infamous example of this was in September 1864, when Sherman's troops set fire to it as they were beginning their march to the sea during the Civil War. At that point, the city was not much more than the confluence of rail lines which made it an important transportation hub. Now three major Interstates converge in downtown Atlanta and its airport is the busiest in the country. In his speech, The New South, Henry W. Grady extolled the virtues of Atlanta, "...we have built a brave and beautiful city; ...somehow or other we have caught the sunshine in the bricks and mortar of our homes and have builded therein not one ignoble prejudice or memory." Very good propaganda for northern financiers looking for reliable investments. It also highlights Atlanta's place as a slightly different southern metropolis, the cultural and economic regional hub it would be for the next hundred plus years. Looking at archival photos of Atlanta throughout its history, one is immediately struck by its radical transformation throughout time; from the railroad lines which gave Five Points its name to the sprawling economic center which gobbled up its former suburbs as it expanded. When I was in high school, people in Marietta and Sandy Springs bristled if one said they were from Atlanta and now people born there regularly claim to be natives. With the influx of outside the perimeter (OTP) folks into town, not to mention transplants and immigrants from all over, the development of the Beltline, and the rise of the film industry in Georgia, the only constant in Atlanta is change.

Icons

Though we both existed on the planet together for about five years, I have no living memory of Martin Luther King. He was assassinated sixteen days before my fifth birthday. I recall hearing of his assassination at the time it happened, but I do not recall specifically how I heard about it, nor did I understand or appreciate what it meant.

My mother, father, or grandmother clarified who he was. I had no frame of reference for what they told me, however, and I also don't recall the reaction, if any, news of his death elicited among them. Given the conservative leanings of my family, I imagine they were not heavily invested in the Civil Rights movement.

As the years have passed, and the people who knew him best have left the scene, the historic King has slowly faded into the shadows of history. In his place is the iconic MLK, a man of perfect wisdom and humility, who held a mirror to society to show us its dark side. I wonder what the actual man would think of how he's been remembered? I surmise that he would be happy to know so much of his message has survived, though he might also be frustrated at how much has been reinterpreted by politicians and others promoting their own agendas and by how much work remains to be accomplished half a century after his death.

In the first century of the so-called "Christian era", a Jewish Messianic contender called Yeshua Bar Abbas led a revolt against Imperial Rome and was crucified for it. His followers believed God would raise him from the dead, and may have stolen his body from its tomb. The world remembers him as Jesus Christ, a dying and resurrected savior king at the center of a Pagan mystery cult. Whenever the historic figure fell short of the icon, the icon always won out, until very little of the historic figure remains.

We are a species obsessed with icons, ideals of what we should be rather than what we are, an advanced group of higher primates. The reality always falls short of the icon, and yet, it's the reality with which we must contend.

Communication Breakdown

The Internet was once solely the province of academics and researchers; universities communicating with the governmental and military facilities that financed their research, and governmental and military facilities communicating with one another. The type of information it carried was static and highly structured and, since unhindered communication was a necessity, there were few boundaries, and the people using it were expected to know and abide by its rules. As a result, there was little need for security and facilities routinely shared information and files. The very purpose of the Internet was the free exchange of information, laying the groundwork for the massive communications portal it has become

As college students found their way onto the Internet, this culture began to change. The type of information exchanged became more informal and less rigid. Newsgroups began to flourish where people could chat, exchange information, and occasionally seek out nude photos of popular celebrities. It was in this environment where I first discovered the Internet, through an account at New York University, sometime around 1993. At the time, Freenets were springing up at places like Case Western University in Cleveland, and Erlangen in Germany which represented some of the earliest attempts to establish online Internet communities — sort of like Facebook without all the ads or monitoring. The first note I posted to an Internet newsgroup was an inquiry about my family on soc.genealogy, and the first response I received was from a guy in Australia, telling me there were Lupos Down Under.

America Online (AOL) was one of the first widespread attempts by a company to package Internet usage and sell it to consumers with no background in the technology. Throughout the mid-1990s, their ubiquitous compact disks provided many experienced Internet users with free coasters for their drinks while allowing novice users their first access to the freewheeling and anarchistic world of the Internet, and most didn't like what they found there. Many of these people had backgrounds in the rigidly structured world of online services such as Prodigy and found it hard to deal with a platform with no centralized authority which, to many, must have resembled an unmonitored bulletin board at their local supermarket.

It was during this period when the Internet was being overrun by one group of newcomers after another that I began to see it as a microcosm of society at large, particularly with regards to the experience of immigrants. Each new group started with zero knowledge of the existing protocols and etiquette, and usually set off a backlash among more seasoned users, in particular, those who had themselves been newcomers just a few years earlier.

When students started using the Internet, the systems administrators who kept the mechanisms functioning, and therefore had the highest degree of knowledge about the portal, found themselves dealing with less experienced people who wanted to set up numerous chat rooms and newsgroups which, in the eyes of the admins, wasted bandwidth. The students, who established the rudimentary elements of what would over the next two decades evolve into social media, resented the intrusion of the first wave of consumers onto the Internet via services such as Netcom and AOL, especially since this included many of their parents, and the term "AOLuser" became a favorite derogatory expression for them. WebTV made it even easier for inexperienced people to get on the Internet, invoking the ire of AOL users, who now considered themselves the experts, just as the Anglo-Saxon inhabitants of cities such as New York and Boston resented the influx of Irish, German, Italian, and Jewish immigrants in the late-19th and early-20th centuries, and as many descendants of those newcomers are now resentful of Muslim or South American arrivals.

When the World Wide Web first came about in the early-90s, I didn't like it. Unix browsers at the time were text based without a method for displaying graphics and the whole enterprise seemed designed as a method of collecting links to other sites rather than conveying useful information. Netscape changed all that. The introduction of a graphical interface to the web suddenly made it come to life and demonstrated its full potential for transmitting knowledge. The Hypertext Markup Language (HTML) which made up the web was a simplified form of Standard General Markup Language (SGML) used at CERN, making it relatively easy to master. Before long, websites were popping up all over the place, and businesses were anxious to get pages set up, even if they didn't understand what the Web was or why they needed to be there. Many of these early pages were little more that fact sheets about the company containing text, with some photos, and a phone number or email link to contact a representative.

The Internet has since become a giant, worldwide, around the clock conversation that anyone with access is free to take part in. Implicit in that, however, is figuring out the rules, and observing the etiquette necessary to get the most out of the experience. Learning to navigate the various social media platforms is akin to learning a new language and culture. Each one has its own customs and quirks, and therefore its own special flavor. For people who spend most of their time on Facebook, visiting Reddit might be a confusing experience, and a considerable learning curve could be needed to understand the culture. Going from WordPress to Twitter would be similar to a novelist switching to writing micro stories. Instagram does not support animated GIFs, whereas Tumblr seems to thrive on them. Nowadays, the free transmission of information, which was the bedrock of the early Internet, has led to such problems as identity theft, denial of service attacks, and phishing scams making tighter security a necessity.

Security is not the only dark side of the Internet. One industry which has thrived has been the porno industry. With the advent of digital cameras and video recorders, and quick wireless connections, filmmakers only need a reliable server, a domain name and willing participants to set up shop. It is, perhaps, typically human to create the most advanced communication network ever devised then use it to download and view nude photos and sexually explicit videos. On a more sinister note, terrorist networks such as ISIL use the Internet to communicate quickly, and to recruit new members.

An even more pervasive threat is cyber bullying and online shaming. Anyone who has ever visited certain Reddit forums, or read the comments on a news or political site, knows of the incendiary nature of some of the posts. Marginalization within society which breeds hostility and mistrust, combined with the relative anonymity of online forums, combine to contribute to the angry and twisted posts some people make. Cyber bullies on the Internet have adopted the tactics of anti-abortion activists of the nineties, conducting all out warfare against those they perceive as deserving of their scorn. Access to information and the number of public records available make it easy to identify and track an individual and just as easy to post personal details which "go viral" and disseminate quickly. As an experiment, I once tried collecting facts on an individual whose name I overheard at an event the previous evening and the level of knowledge I was able to gain about the person was frightening. In the hands of cyber vigilantes, and an overly eager audience numbering in the millions, information can become a deadly weapon.

Free exchange of information via the Internet has had a profound effect on people in the late 20th and early 21st centuries. Throughout Africa, for instance, people use their phones to share music and videos of their favorite local bands or performers, giving them a global audience. It's almost a cliché within the United States to see people glued to their wireless devices, oblivious to the world around them. With technology advancing at an increasing pace, the information revolution created by the Internet and World Wide Web in the 1990s, seems destined to transform society for generations to come.

Summer of 1996

For seventeen days in the summer of 1996, Atlanta became a mirror image of itself, where the downtown connector was clear, MARTA was packed, and the world stopped by for a visit. Less than a year before, Atlanta had been thrilled when the Braves brought home their first and only World Series pennant since coming to town, so spirits were high as '96 dawned. Atlanta had worked hard to get the Olympics, under the watchful eye of the Atlanta Committee for the Olympic Games (ACOG). They were responsible for everything from seeing that the city was ready for the influx of international athletes and spectators, to giving the Atlanta Games the worst mascot in the history of sports up to that point, in the form of Whatizit, or Izzy, the blue blob in sneakers which had absolutely nothing to do with the city's past, present, or future. The Paralympics, held a month or so afterward in the same venues, had, as their mascot, Blaze, which was based on Atlanta's symbol, the Phoenix, thus proving someone cared about getting things right.

At the time of the Olympics, I was Membership Vice President for the Atlanta Junior Chamber of Commerce, or Jaycees. Like everyone else, our activities were hampered by events around town so we contented ourselves with accomplishing what we could while taking in as much of the Games as possible. I apparently tried to get a job working concessions at one of the venues, as I have an ID badge from Aramark, which I never surrendered, as instructions on the back say I should have. I remember going downtown to ACOG headquarters to get the ID but don't recall why I didn't follow through on the job. It's possible it was a volunteer fundraising opportunity for the Jaycees — where we worked, and the organization got paid — that didn't work out.

Authorities had been warning residents of potential traffic problems for months ahead of the Games, so the terrifying specter of twenty-four-hour gridlock haunted the waking hours of most commuters. The reality was much different than what had been foretold, as suburbanites, frightened into not driving, crowded onto MARTA, leaving the highways far less crammed. I lived in East Point at the time and had to commute through town to North Druid Hills for work, and to say I was pleasantly surprised to encounter rush hour traffic in downtown Atlanta moving fifty-five to sixty miles an hour is putting it mildly. Driving through town I passed the Olympic Stadium every morning and evening, making it one of the few times I've driven in town as an adult where I actually enjoyed the trip.

The relationship between city government, ACOG, and the International Olympic Committee was often tense. A number of construction projects were being finished just as Olympic officials started arriving and news reports were full of stories about haughty officials or their families demanding special treatment or otherwise being rude. Other countries' delegations complained about the rampant patriotism on display at venues, particularly the indoor gymnastics events, where deafening chants of "USA, USA!" made it difficult for athletes to concentrate. Despite all the hiccups, the mood around Atlanta was festive and lighthearted as everyone looked forward to putting on the best Games ever.

All that changed on the evening of 27 July when a bomb went off in Centennial Park, killing or contributing to the deaths of two people and injuring a hundred and eleven. The death toll might have been much higher, had it not been for the actions of a sharp-eyed security guard named Richard Jewell. While 911 operators argued over the address of Centennial Park after receiving an anonymous bomb threat, Jewell spotted a suspicious backpack, notified his superiors and began evacuating the area. His reward for what may have been the most remarkable achievement of his career was to be crucified in the press after an overzealous FBI leaked his name as a suspect. While he won a court case against the news network whose reporting did the most damage and was eventually vindicated with the arrest and conviction of Eric Rudolph some years later, it's doubtful his reputation ever fully recovered. He died on 29 August 2007 at age forty-four.

The morning after the attack, I had a ticket to see Olympic tennis at Stone Mountain. I woke up, dressed, and hopped on MARTA without turning on the television, and did not learn of the details of the bombing until I arrived at Kensington MARTA station and saw the front page of the Atlanta Journal/Constitution. There had been rumblings along the way of beefed up security, due to an incident, but I didn't learn the full extent of it until I saw the paper.

In addition to that one morning of tennis which stretched into late afternoon due to several lengthy rain delays, and which featured Andre Agassi and Monica Seles, other events I attended included one night of track and field at Olympic Stadium, and one afternoon when I drove to Athens to see the finals of rhythmic gymnastics. I had been invited by a colleague to see the first match-up of the US versus Cuba in baseball, but we failed to hook up at the venue and since he had the tickets, I couldn't get in.

Before the Games began, I managed to see the torch relay at three separate locations around town but only specifically recall two of them, one evening with some friends on Roswell Road, and once on Clifton Road in the afternoon, in front of the CDC, where I was working. Someone who worked on my floor was one of the torch bearers and I was able to have a picture taken with the torch. I believe the third was on Peachtree Street close to the intersection of West Peachtree, near where the Jaycees had their office. This one was by chance, as I'd gone to the location for another purpose and just happened to find myself in close proximity to the relay.

One of the enduring landmarks from the Games is the statue in Midtown just above the intersection of Peachtree and West Peachtree, identified as "The World Athletes Monument", donated to the city by a trust run by Prince Charles. I've always referred to it as "The Statue of Five Naked Guys Holding Up the Globe that Prince Charles Gave Us During the Olympics". A few years later, when Princess Diana was killed in a car accident, the statue became the focal point in town for remembrances of her, which is ironic considering she and Charles had been divorced for a number of years by that point.

There were numerous other arts projects during the Games, part of the Cultural Olympiad which coincided with the Games. Plays were written and performed, statues erected, giant murals were painted, many of which were painted over or demolished when the buildings on which they were painted were torn down to make room for something else. There are, still, a few remnants of the Games around, Centennial Park and Turner Field the most visible, but many of the venues were broken down, packed up and shipped elsewhere once the Paralympics were over. To finance the building of Centennial Park, ACOG sold bricks where one could have his or her name imprinted. I purchased one in memory of my father, who died in April 1995. The brick is located in Section 63, making it easier for me to remember where it is, as that's the year I was born.

The Atlanta Jaycees had a membership meet and greet scheduled for Lulu's Bait Shack in Buckhead for the Tuesday after the

Olympics closed which evolved into our "Farewell to the World" party. That Tuesday evening in Buckhead felt more like a Friday or Saturday, as residents who'd had to stay home to avoid the traffic and hassles of having the Games in town turned out to let off steam once they were gone. A festive atmosphere was evident as we reveled in the fact that we'd survived it all. It must have been reminiscent of how folks reacted when Sherman packed up and headed off to Savannah in 1864, notwithstanding the fact that for us, most of the city was still intact which was one thing for which we were all grateful.

What Nature Intended

In Genesis, the first humans are instructed to be fruitful and multiply. Given that the human population now exceeds seven billion individuals, one could assume humans took that instruction to heart. Along the way, the transition from hunter gathers, where the population was constantly on the move, to an agrarian society where everyone stays put, no doubt helped humans in this goal. Development of technology and industry, advances in medicine, and improvements in our diet also played a part, and for that, we have our advanced brains to thank. Had our ancestors not begun to walk upright, which freed their hands to allow for tool making, which, in turn led to the development of our brains, we might still be swinging in trees, rather than building skyscrapers, unraveling our genetic code, and planning a trip to Mars. We have done such a good job of distancing ourselves from our primate past that we've created numerous myths of divine origin to explain where we came from rather than accepting what the evolutionary evidence tells us.

In the film The Adventures of Baron Munchausen, Robin Williams plays a king who can detach his head from his body. Connected he's course and vile, and enslaved by his animal instincts, but detached, he's thoughtful and contemplative and fully intellectual. Many people like to believe humans operate as essentially rational creatures, guided by common sense, and ignore the many, many times we behave in ways contrary to rational behavior. Nowhere is this more evident than in the area of attraction and the dating rituals we devise for finding and choosing a mate.

The religious sect known as the Shakers was an example of a community who practiced celibacy, even between married couples, and chose to grow by recruiting new members rather than via the traditional route of having children. They found alternate means, such as weird dances and building distinctive furniture, as a way of channeling their creative impulses away from their sexual desires and, as a result, all that remains of their community, aside from a few later converts who may still practice the lifestyle, is the furniture they created. The sect went extinct when the last of its stalwarts died off during the twentieth century. I've read that the Gnostics also had a disdain for sexual contact, choosing to focus on the mind over the body, which may have contributed to their decline.

Typically, the higher up the economic ladder one moves, the fewer children one has. In an agrarian society where many individuals are needed to perform the necessary work, larger family sizes are advantageous to create the workforce a family would require. In my genealogical work, I've seen families with as many as eighteen to twenty children, though not all by the same mother. For those living in cramped urban settings, large families are less of an advantage, though they can be found there as well, particularly among immigrants. Equally so, given the risks inherent in childbearing, expecting one woman to bear numerous children over a relatively short period of time can be dangerous for both the woman and her offspring. There's a reason why the mortality rate for women and infants was so high in colonial times besides the lack of adequate pre- and postnatal care available.

In patriarchal societies, fathers or other male relatives choose how women will be joined with their mates, and often the strongest and most influential men get first choice, surprise, surprise. In much of nature, however, it's the female of the species which makes that choice, and the males must put on elaborate displays to attract the attention of willing partners. If one sees a pair of cardinals, for instance, the one most brilliantly arrayed is the male, and among songbirds, it's often the males who sing elaborate songs in order to attract mates. In cultures which tend to be matriarchal, we also see this behavior in humans, males prancing and preening in makeup and brightly colored costumes to attract the attention of their intended brides. Given the vastly different roles played by males and females in reproduction, particularly with mammals, it makes more sense for the female to choose, since she's taking the greater risk in getting pregnant. Even in patriarchal societies we see vestiges of this, fathers choosing their daughters' husbands based on who will best provide for them, or which tribal alliances will best insure their survival.

While a change in thinking can alter the desire to have children, we have yet to overcome a simple fact of reproduction. In order for there to be a child, there has to be a contribution from a man and a woman regardless of whether the two have sex. Neither gender can produce a child solely on its own. There has been talk of fusing genes or chromosomes, or otherwise cloning a person to overcome this situation, but as of now, science has yet to produce a human child using this method. The fundamentalist claim that homosexuals can't reproduce doesn't take into account the fact that both parents no longer need to be present at the moment of conception.

For someone trying to reason out why people behave the way they do, homosexuality may seem like an anomaly. Two men together or two women together cannot produce a child, and since the biological imperative for all creatures on earth seems to be to survive and procreate, homosexuality doesn't appear to play a role in that. For someone who adheres to a philosophy which states that all life was fashioned in the image of a divine creator, people frequently come to the conclusion that homosexuality is against the design of this creator, and yet, humans are not the only species to exhibit such behavior, we're just the only ones who constantly obsess over it. Remove divine intent from the equation, and we're still left with the quandary of figuring out what, if any, evolutionary function homosexuality serves. The problem is we're most likely still overthinking it.

When discussing human behavior, particularly with regard to sexuality, one often speaks of "what nature intended", and yet, we rarely speak of this when talking about other natural phenomena. If a region is hit by an earthquake or flood, the people there usually don't interpret that as nature telling them they don't belong there, though insurance companies might disagree. It's only in the realm of human behavior that we assume some divine purpose underlies what we do. Trying to figure out why something happens is usually the first step in figuring out how to prevent something from happening, and more than a few people throughout the world would be happy if homosexuality could be eliminated. The question is why?

One cannot simply look at a person and know that person's sexuality. Men and women who don't meet society's standards for masculinity and femininity still choose mates of the opposite sex, while people who conform to the behaviors assigned by society for that gender sometimes don't. We have seen numerous instances of very masculine male athletes coming out as gay, and feminine models and actresses announcing they're lesbians. As homosexuality becomes less stigmatized in society, we'll undoubtedly have more people inclined to identify as such. We don't even need high profile illustrations, since pretty much everyone knows someone they thought was or wasn't gay up until the time that person started dating someone of the same or opposite sex. As with many things in nature, there doesn't appear to be any rhyme or reason to it. It's society and culture that typically complicates things and we're responsible for developing and maintaining those.

So, what did nature intend in creating homosexuality? Most likely nothing. With regard to biology, nature is usually a passive force which sometimes gives species mutations that have no effect on survival unless conditions exist that make that mutation an advantage. The way a given species reproduces is the result of billions of years of evolution and the fact that different species have vastly different methods of reproduction suggests no specific plan was in place from the start. One might argue that homosexuality is one of the curbs that nature puts in place to control population growth, but this ignores two important facts. First, the percentage of people who exclusively identify as homosexual in society appears to remain constant while the population gets larger. Second, and more importantly, people who are homosexual are still capable of having children. Neither the ability nor the desire to have children is affected by one's sexual preference. True, there are many homosexuals who don't want children, but there is probably an equal percentage of heterosexuals who also don't wish to be parents. If there is a curb, it's the lack of desire to reproduce rather than the type of relationship one is in that makes the difference.

Societal prohibitions against homosexuals focus almost exclusively on male homosexuality. Leviticus 18 forbids men from having sex with other men and says nothing about women. It's not until much later that admonitions for women were added to Jewish law. It's likely the restriction was put in place because this was behavior observed in cultures with whom the ancient Israelites interacted. It's known that the ancient Greeks practiced homosexuality, though the specific cultural context is probably lost to us today. It would seem then, that the prohibition has less to do with protecting families or society than with controlling a specific type of male behavior.

Throughout human populations, rape is often a powerful weapon employed in asserting control over other individuals or groups of people. Despite its sexual nature, rape is not about sex, but about demonstrating one's dominance over another person. In Western society, males who are raped by other males often carry a higher stigma than females who've been raped, and boys who've been sexually abused often receive more attention than girls. Aside from totally ignoring or flippantly dismissing rape allegations by women, authorities take male rape very seriously, believing it diminishes the man's masculinity. One rarely hears someone dismiss allegations of rape by one man against another with the phrase, "Boys will be boys" though anecdotal evidence from prisons and other male-dominated endeavors tell a different story. Despite the fear mongering by anti-gay activists, men who rape other men often do not identify as homosexuals, since, again, rape is not about sexuality, but control.

So, it seems the real culprit is not human sexuality, but the need by humans to exert control over others, and that is a perversion of the survival instinct, since those who control the resources have a better chance to survive than those who don't. We see, in parts of Africa where water and other natural resources are scarce, the highest level of strife, as populations are constantly at odds to try to claim those resources. In the Balkans, while the Soviet Union was still in place, people of different ethnicities lived side by side with relatively little conflict, but once the stabilizing influence of an authoritarian regime was removed, ethnic cleansing soon followed.

The challenge for us is not to eliminate homosexuality from existence, since its presence has not proven detrimental to the health and welfare of our society. Rather it's to overcome the need for humans to exert dominance over their environment and fellow individuals, which has been shown to hinder growth and development, bringing about such atrocities as wartime sexual violence and genocide, and leading to such repressive regimes as Apartheid-era South Africa. Our focus, then, should not be on those who wish to lead contented lives with partners they desire, but rather those who'll stop at nothing to prevent them.

Origin Stories

"In the beginning God created the heavens and the earth." So begins the first creation narrative in Genesis, chapter one. This narrative, which among other things states that water existed on earth before there was light, encompasses the creation of all living things, including humans. The story is directly contradicted by the following chapter of Genesis, which states that the human race sprang from a single man created out of mud and his female companion who was created from one of the man's ribs, and that all animals were created after the man to be his companions.

Science has given us the idea of the Big Bang as event one in the origin of the universe, but there seems to be no unified agreement on what came before or specifically what caused it. Modern space exploration has yet to reveal much about the first few moments following the Big Bang when many important developments are thought to have occurred. Ancient Eastern philosophies postulate an expanding and contracting universe which seems to agree somewhat with modern science, though couched in their own religious language, the days and nights of Brahma.

If we are to believe the universe was spoken into existence by God, we could just as easily surmise that all existence is nothing more than an illusion in the mind of God, since God would only need to think of something to bring it into existence. The world we inhabit has substance, however, and the elements can be broken down into smaller units. We don't just see and hear the world; we can touch it, taste and smell it. If we're just illusions within the mind of God we're part of an extremely intricate illusion. If the account in Genesis is correct, and the earth was spoken into existence six thousand years ago, undoubtedly there had to be an intelligent entity there to guide how it turned out, given its current advanced state. If the world is several billion years old as scientific evidence suggests, that leaves a lot of time for trial and error.

Creation follows a logical sequence; no one builds a house from the inside out. First, the foundation is laid, then the frame is constructed, then the walls and ceilings are put in place. Before life as we know it could develop on earth there had to be water. Before there could be water, the elements of hydrogen and oxygen had to exist. Prior to that, at some point early in the origin of the universe, matter and energy were instilled with certain properties, which led to everything that came afterward. Was this part of a conscious plan by an intelligent entity? Humans have attempted to answer that question for as long as they've had minds with which to ponder the nature of the universe. If the earth began as a fiery mass spinning in the cosmos before settling into orbit around the sun, it had to cool down considerably so the elements could come together to create water and develop an atmosphere. This most likely didn't happen in six days.

Most apes live in trees. One day, one of them came down and decided to go for a walk. The ultimate outcome was the human race. As origin stories go, it's not the most detailed or dramatic, but may be closer to what actually happened, though the process probably took millions of years. In much of the material I've read, many scientists do believe walking upright was the biological innovation that freed up humans' hands and allowed them to become the toolmakers that gave them their competitive advantages in the wild. Toolmaking helped them to develop their advanced brains, which eventually led to language.

If we look at the development of a child, we can get a rough idea of how humans probably developed. At first, the child is totally helpless, before learning to move its arms and legs, to manipulate objects, and to stand. Next, the child learns to crawl, then walk, and at last acquires language. By age four or five, a person has acquired sufficient mobility to carry out most tasks but lacks the proper level of maturity to survive on his or her own. Using the analogy of an individual, I would estimate that the human race is just entering puberty.

Everything has a beginning. Sometimes we're fortunate enough to be present when something starts. Within my lifetime, much of current day Atlanta has been built and, in many cases, demolished and replaced by something bigger but not always better. For those events we weren't present to witness first hand, all we have is the evidence left behind. It's how we interpret the clues that leads us to our own origin stories.

Foot Soldiers in the War on Xmas

Every Christmas season, alongside numerous productions of *A Christmas Carol*, someone in the media will raise the specter of a "War on Christmas!" One pundit has made it his stock in trade to lament how every season more Christmas traditions are under fire, driving Christians underground in their observance, lest the politically correct thought police kick down their doors and cart them off to re-education camps where they quickly learn to say "Happy Holidays" or else. To the best of my knowledge, no one in the US has ever been arrested for wishing someone "Merry Christmas" and unless one attends a mosque in Texas, it's unlikely armed vigilantes will station themselves outside one's place of worship to disrupt the practice of one's faith.

The notion of there being a war on Christmas is nothing new. I recall a song from the 70s or 80s where the singer told listeners "Don't wish me Merry Xmas," and as a child, I frequently heard grownups railing against people who abbreviated the holiday in this manner. Use of an X in place of the word "Christ" is not a modern phenomenon, however; it was a traditional method of abbreviating the name, dating back hundreds of years, even showing up in parish registers in England in the sixteenth century and in early Colonial wills and administrations. In some old documents I've seen, for instance, the name "Christopher" is sometimes rendered as "Xopher". The English X represents the Greek letter Chi, which is the first letter in the name of Christ in the original Greek versions of the New Testament. When combined with the Rho symbol, which looks like a P, the result is an abbreviation of Jesus' name, XP with the X superimposed over the P.

Growing up in the Methodist church, I was constantly warned that anti-Christian forces were clamoring at the gates, anxious to take away all our observances and impose their Pagan ways on true believers. Interestingly enough, Christmas started out as a Pagan feast day commemorating the Winter solstice, that was adopted by the early church to make the transition to Christianity more palatable to Pagan converts. People may be flexible on the deity, but they aren't so willing to give up their elaborate feasts in observance of it.

One of the earliest wars on Christmas, in fact, was conducted by Puritans in the US who refused to observe the holiday precisely because of its Pagan origins. Most Christian sects in the colonies were Protestant, so Christmas wasn't celebrated in its traditional form for at least two centuries after the first English settlers arrived. It wasn't until the late-19th and early-20th centuries that the holiday we now celebrate began to gain in popularity. Works like Charles Dickens' *A Christmas Carol*, and "A Visit from St. Nicholas" by Clement C. Moore helped to revive interest in it.

If any holiday in the US is under attack, it's Thanksgiving, which is increasingly overlooked in the weeks between Halloween and Black Friday. As it stands, many simply regard it as a day to watch football and eat too much. Retailers, in collusion with the media, have turned this truly American observance into little more than Black Friday's Eve in the rush to start the Christmas season and get people spending money. Stores, which were once closed on Thanksgiving, now open late in the day to lure in early shoppers and the focus is always on who'll be camping out at stores that night to get the best values the following morning rather than on being grateful for the good fortune one has experienced throughout the year.

Wishing someone "Happy Holidays" instead of "Merry Christmas" need not diminish one's enjoyment of the season, and in fact, it's usually companies and not individuals who are expected to be accommodating in this manner. It is merely an acknowledgement of the fact that we live in a diverse society where not everyone follows the same customs. Despite the ire of many pundits on television and radio, this is actually a good thing. Diversity should be celebrated as it is the sign of a healthy and vibrant society. Plenty of people still say, "Merry Christmas" and I've yet to hear of any of them losing their jobs or disappearing in the middle of the night because of it. If one is assured in one's faith, tolerance of other people's beliefs should not represent a threat.

To foster the notion of a war on Christmas means there must be forces conducting this war and holding this belief accomplishes little more than to set one community of faith against another. There's enough hostility in the world without inventing reasons for more. Despite one's religious background, or lack thereof, the idea of peace on earth and good will towards all is a notion we should each strive to embrace.

Dead Parrots and Shows about Nothing

People think of absurdity as someone acting irrationally, or strange things happening to an otherwise normal person, but often the heart of absurdity lies in people rationalizing behavior which defies explanation. My stock portfolio just tanked; now's the perfect time to buy more! Whenever our instincts conflict with our intellects, we're often at a loss to explain the discrepancy and grasp for whatever explanation seems to best suit the situation, regardless of how convoluted the logic may be. Writers such as Albert Camus have explored the absurdities of human behavior — the struggle to find meaning in an otherwise chaotic universe where events often seem random and arbitrary. For Camus, the ultimate absurdist act was suicide, particularly in reaction to the meaningless of existence.

The human compulsion to create rules, only to search for ways to bend or break them provides endless examples of absurdist logic in action. While the tendency to make inexplicable decisions sometimes defies common sense, there is, often, a logic to absurdist reasoning, even if the reasons defy convention or otherwise seem contrived. A good source for examples of this is the Book of Job in the Bible, where Job must endure numerous hardships, including physical maladies and the deaths of loved ones, for no other reason than God wanting to demonstrate to Satan how righteous Job is.

On the iconic television show Seinfeld, the absurdity sprang from the fact that the main characters knew their method of dealing with life often hurt them but were unable or unwilling to change. Other commentators have pointed out how unlikable the characters were: Jerry the self-centered perfectionist; Elaine the insufferable intellectual snob; George the pathological liar; Kramer the bumbling n'er-do-well who often succeeds in spite of himself. What is most apparent about each of these characters is how often their problems are caused or escalated by their refusal to alter their behavior, even when that behavior is shown to have negative consequences. This was best highlighted in the episode entitled The Opposite, where George started doing the opposite of what his instincts told him, and soon found his dream job, an attractive girlfriend, and the success which had long eluded him.

A forerunner of the absurdity implicit in Seinfeld was the legendary British show Monty Python's Flying Circus, which introduced the antics of John Cleese, Michael Palin, Graham Chapman, Eric Idle, Terry Jones and Terry Gilliam to audiences in the United States, and befuddled numerous Silent Generation parents. The absurdity of Python often derived from distinguished people doing silly things; proper British upper crust individuals acting like idiots. With Python, it was common to establish a theme early in the show which keeps recurring throughout, such as a segment on identifying trees that only seemed to highlight "the larch" or having characters randomly say, in utter confusion, "lemon curry?" Seinfeld also had such themes, such as when George gets in trouble for saying "Bless you" when someone sneezes. Jerry proposes replacing the phrase with, "You are so good looking," establishing the running gag for that episode.

One of the most famous sketches on Monty Python was The Pet Shop or, as it's better known, the dead parrot sketch. John Cleese portrays a disgruntled customer returning to a pet shop with a parrot he purchased which he's discovered is dead. The outright absurdity of the customer trying to convince the shop keeper of the condition of the parrot is compounded by the revelation during the skit that the bird was apparently dead when sold to the customer. What is instantly recognizable is not only how ridiculous the situation is, but how true to life it is. Who among us has not had to deal with a know-it-all salesperson whose eye toward the next transaction overrides his or her concern in helping the customer? Is Cleese's indignation at being "had" any different than a shopper's ire over being sold a substitute pair of shoes that do not fit well, or learning that the advertised deal which lures people into a store is not available and most likely never was?

What often made Seinfeld so interesting was how densely packed it could be. In the episode called The Pothole, each of the main characters had storylines, and even Newman had a subplot related to the main action. Jerry accidentally knocks his girlfriend's toothbrush into the toilet, and she uses it before he has a chance to tell her; George loses a key chain given to him by his boss; Elaine tries to devise a way to order Chinese takeout despite living on the wrong side of the street; and Kramer adopts a highway. In this episode, the worst tendencies of each character were fully on display. How else could it end than in a fiery cataclysm?

For centuries, it has been the province of drama and literature to point out the foibles of human nature and thus hold a mirror up to the behavior of individuals with an eye toward instructing them in proper actions. The Greek tragedies were filled with the consequences of failing to heed the will of the gods, and medieval morality plays featured stock characters with whom the audience could identify, often led astray by their baser instincts.

In Job, his three friends try to convince him his fortune will improve if he'll only admit that he's not as righteous as he claims. Job protests that he's done nothing wrong and the reader knows he's telling the truth. Throughout, Job's speeches have a sarcastic ring to them leading one to believe the writer's intent was to be darkly humorous. If Job doesn't represent the birth of absurdist literature, it's certainly one if the earliest surviving examples of it.

Even the most absurd situations have a logic to them. In my comedy sketch Got Your Goat, a man named Harold comes home to his high-rise condo in Midtown Atlanta and asks his flustered wife, Agnes, where the goats are. After a bit of conversation back and forth Agnes confirms that Harold isn't crazy, they really do have goats. While the surface situation is absurd, underlying it is the logical premise that Harold has a familiar ritual in his life which brings him solace and when it isn't there, he doesn't accept the loss easily or well.

Whether it's the contrived silliness of Monty Python or the situational absurdity of Seinfeld, the humor presented resonates with audiences from one generation to the next. Perhaps the impact of Seinfeld was its instructive nature, displaying the petty and superficial actions of its characters as a mirror on the narcissistic and self-serving culture of the nineties, warning viewers against becoming too self-involved. As with previous generations, tracing back through the morality plays, the Greek tragedies, and the Book of Job, it's a lesson people need to be reminded of again and again.

The Book of Job

The Book of Job takes the form of a dialogue between Job and his three friends, Eliphaz the Temanite, Bildad the Shuhite, and Zophar the Naamathite. Along the way, we also hear from Elihu, who's identified as the son of Barakel the Buzite. At the end, God steps in and communicates with Job as well. The story goes on for forty-two chapters, and it's only in the first two that it's explained why Job and his friends are having the conversation. In Chapters 1 and 2, described in the New International Version (NIV) of the Bible, as "The Prologue," we're told that the sons of God and Satan are hanging out, when God shows up, and starts bragging to Satan about how righteous Job is. Satan contends that anyone will praise God when things are going well, but not so much when things are going badly, so God tells Satan to rain down all manner of punishment on Job, to demonstrate that Job will not forsake God. In the first chapter, Job loses his house, his livestock, seven sons, and three daughters, in rapid succession. In the second chapter, God allows Satan to afflict Job with sores over his entire body.

This is one of the stories where it's worth noting the differences in translations to describe the entities that have gathered at the beginning, and it demonstrates how the translation can alter the meaning of the text, sometimes significantly. The NIV refers to "angels" gathering before God but explains in a footnote that in the original Hebrew, the term "sons of God" is used. The New American Standard Bible, and the King James Version, among others, identify them as "sons of God." The International Standard Version uses "divine beings," and the Good News Translation calls them "heavenly beings." Earlier, in the story of Noah in Genesis, the NIV mentions the "sons of God" without translating the term as angels. It is an extremely important distinction, especially since Satan is counted among these entities, though a footnote in the NIV explains that "Satan" means "adversary" without specifying whose adversary. God doesn't seem surprised to see Satan hanging around, and their conversation does not imply a great deal of animosity between them.

The story of Job presents us with an atypical biblical protagonist, because no attempt is made to tie Job to any of the known patriarchs or tribes of the Israelites; all we're told is that he lives in the land of Uz, probably in Persia or Babylon. In fact, we're not told how Job is connected to the Israelites at all, or where in the history of Israel his story takes place, and none of his friends appear to be connected to them either. They're identified by their tribal designation, but only one, the Temanites are mentioned elsewhere in the Bible, in two identical references in Genesis and 1 Chronicles. In the extensive genealogies that begin 1 Chronicles, one of Esau's sons is identified as Eliphaz, and he's listed as the father of Teman, presumably the progenitor of the Temanites, but other than that, no other mention has been found. The name Elihu shows up in 1 Samuel and 1 Chronicles, but these do not appear to be the same Elihu as in the story of Job.

The Asbury Bible Commentary found at The Bible Gateway (biblegateway.com) places Job within the "Wisdom literature" which includes Psalms and Proverbs. It's likely this story came from one of the cultures with whom the Israelites interacted, and was adapted for use in the Hebrew Bible as were other works such as the Book of Esther which bears striking similarities to the Babylonian myth of Ishtar.

Most of the work is told in verse form and consists of a series of long monologues by Job, one of his three friends, Elihu, or God. This is also unusual and suggests the text might have been originally meant to be spoken, perhaps even performed as a play. The structure of Job suggests that chapters 1 and 2, and the brief wrap ups in chapters 32 and 42 were added later by an editor to clarify the action of the narrative. Job's attitude in dealing with his wife in Chapter 2 also differs from his attitude throughout the rest of the piece, though that could be related to the length of his suffering. The dialogue begins after all the calamity has befallen Job, and ends without a resolution, and the prose sections fill in the remainder of the story. The story is presented in the form of a trial; Job delivers his opening statement, each friend cross-examines Job, followed by Job's defense. Elihu's commentary comes after Job makes his final statement, as a sort of amicus brief, and finally, God appears to render a verdict.

Despite its length, Job's tale is reasonably easy to summarize. After Satan is allowed to destroy Job's life without killing him, three of his friends go to him to provide comfort. Job starts out lamenting his fate and wishing God had never allowed him to be born, or that God had killed him while still a baby, so that he'd never have known the suffering that comes from falling out of God's favor. Each of his friends address him, in turn, questioning why Job feels he was righteous, given that the evidence suggests otherwise. The theme that develops is that God doesn't just punish people for no reason, therefore Job must have done something to incur God's wrath. It's important to note that throughout his discussion with his friends, Job is only requesting that he be allowed to state his case before God and does not curse nor blame God. He constantly insists to his friends that he's done nothing to warrant the treatment he's receiving, and readers of the text, who have the benefit of the Prologue, know he's telling the truth.

After Job's friends have had their say and failed to shake Job's conviction in his own blamelessness, Job gives what's identified as his final statement, or closing argument. Once he's finished, Elihu steps forward to offer his thoughts on the matter. Elihu describes himself as much younger than the others and has apparently been on the sidelines listening to the discussion. He says he did not speak up until the three friends made it clear they had finished because they are his elders and he did not wish to interrupt them. Elihu beats around the bush, explaining himself and claiming he's about to say something profound for nearly two chapters before finally getting around to admonishing Job, and he also takes up the theme that God doesn't punish people who don't deserve it. The gist of what Elihu is saying seems to be that no one is more just or righteous than God, which is beside the point, since Job isn't comparing himself to God.

After a few chapters of Elihu, God finally shows up and speaks to Job "out of the storm" which must have come up while Elihu was speaking, since no mention has been made of it before. Elsewhere in the Bible, God is described as speaking from thunder clouds, so perhaps that's what's meant here. In keeping with the stormy theme, God thunders for a few chapters about all the things God can do that Job can't, without really giving Job any real explanation for what's happened to him.

God's rant boils down to "I'm God and you're not", which I'm pretty sure Job already knew without having his property destroyed, his family killed, and his health taken away in the worst possible way. Still, Job knows which side his bread is buttered on, so he agrees with whatever God has to say. Then God berates Job's three friends and confirms everything Job's been saying throughout the whole story. God seems to be angry because the three friends weren't speaking the truth while Job was, and since Job's contention was that God was punishing him for no reason, it seems a very curious admission on God's part.

God then makes all three friends bring Job offerings, and has Job pray for them, since he was right all along. God restores Job's health and fortune, so, of course, all his fair-weather friends and family come back to help him celebrate. The account suggests Job has a rather large extended family, none of whom apparently cared enough about him to take him in when he was in real distress. Whatever else can be said of Eliphaz, Bildad, and Zophar, at least they stuck by Job when he was most in need, even if he didn't find them to be of much comfort to him.

The story ends with the report that Job raised a whole new family to sort of make up for the one that was killed, even though they couldn't. We're told that Job lived to the ripe old age of a hundred and forty, seeing his family to the fourth generation. We're not given any sort of genealogy of Job's descendants, which further isolates Job's story from others which document the children of Israel.

Job's plight raises numerous issues about the nature and intent of God, and it's not clear exactly what readers are meant to take away from how he's treated. First, why is Satan in the presence of God? Wasn't Satan banished to hell for all eternity for the sin of pride? Did Satan get a weekend pass, or time off for good behavior, or was Satan's banishment a later theological development that wasn't known to the author of Job? Also, if Jesus was God's only begotten son, why do multiple translations of the Bible, including the original Hebrew refer to the "sons" of God, here and in Genesis 6 in particular? Since Satan's among them, does that imply Satan was also a son of God? Genesis doesn't just mention that the "sons of God" exist, but that they also interact with humans, taking some of the women as wives.

The Book of Job should leave those who relish the notion of God as a loving father figure with quite a dilemma. Everything that happens to Job happens because God instructs Satan to torment Job. First, God puts Job on Satan's radar, by bragging about how righteous Job is, then when Satan dismisses God's assessment, God allows Satan to harm Job in any way he wants, short of killing him. At any point after Satan starts punishing Job, God could have called the whole thing off, and restored Job to good health and fortune. In the end, God does just that, but while the money and property can be replaced, Job's sons and daughters were killed and they can't be, not even with an all new family. God was fully aware of what was happening, and not only did nothing to stop it, but actually encouraged it all, for no good reason, except, perhaps, to win a bet with Satan.

At other points in the Bible when God acts violently, it's in reaction to something God didn't expect like the Tower of Babel, or basic human nature, but here, God's just being malicious for no reason. Believing it's okay for God to act this way is like saying it's okay for parents to beat their children. It's senseless cruelty, and poor Job is just expected to grin and bear it all, then thank God afterward for teaching him such an important lesson. It should come as no surprise that people who believe in such a God sometimes condone domestic violence, and counsel women to remain in abusive situations for the sake of their families. God should have known what was in Job's heart and mind and should not have been concerned about what Satan had to say on the matter.

The more I read Job, the more convinced I am that it was once meant to be performed, and that its intent was to be darkly humorous or ironic. Modern readers would describe Job's plight as Kafkaesque, in that the tragedies that befall Job do not happen as a result of anything Job has done, and, in fact, he's being punished for being an upstanding and righteous person. Job's rebukes to his friends are very sarcastic, like saying, "With friends like you…" Imagine Job's speeches being read by Jerry Seinfeld or Lewis Black, delivered in their usual acerbic style. Job constantly asserts his innocence and dismay at his misfortune, while his friends cajole him to confess his wrongdoings and beg for mercy from God. Elihu's meandering speech in chapters 32 through 37 comes across as very humorous, like, "Okay, I'm about to talk, any time now. I'm opening my mouth. The words are coming to me. Here they come. Right now. I'm saying 'em." Even God's speech has a humorous tone to it, since it consists of bombastic pronouncements about how great God is.

After insisting for several chapters that God show up so Job can defend himself, when he's finally given the opportunity to address God, all Job does is agree with everything God says, without making much of an issue of it. By that point, who can blame the guy?

Freedom and Consequence

This title was originally published in 2015, though these stories reflect three periods in my development as a writer. *Titania*, *A Bad Day's Work*, *Shocks to the System*, and *Metempsychosis* are from college and graduate school and are set in New York. *The Keys to Success* and *Route 412 to Tulsa* were written and posted to Gather in the mid-oos. *Double Fault*, *Klan Candy*, *The Spitting Spiders of Borneo*, and *Miracle of the Magic Dollar* were written for my blog from 2014 through 2015. The New York stories and *Route 412* were also part of a Kindle edition entitled *Tales of the New Wave*, that I published in 2015 to learn to format work for Kindle. All have been edited extensively since their first appearances.

Titania

And for her sake do I rear up her boy,
And for her sake I will not part with him.
—Shakespeare, *A Midsummer Night's Dream*

Terry walked up Broadway, her hands clenched at her sides, her head down. She shook her head then ran her hand roughly through her short dark hair, and said softly, "That son of a bitch." She shoved her hands into the pockets of her overcoat and tried not to think, but the harder she tried the more she saw his face, heard his words.

"I want my boy."

Terry thought of Madeline and saw her as she was when Terry first met her, wearing an awful, floral print dress and a white shawl. Her shoulder-length black hair was cropped close to her face and she had bright, china-blue eyes.

She was so small. Never would have believed she was over fourteen, but she was already out of college.

Terry had made her usual after-work walk around Battery Park then went to the harbor and that's where she saw Madeline, hands on the railing, head propped on them, looking down into the water. Terry joined her at the railing. From the moment she stopped there, Terry felt she had come under close scrutiny and out of the corner of her eye could see Madeline's head turned toward her. Whenever she looked, however, Madeline was again staring down at the waves. At last, Terry caught her and for a few brief moments their eyes met then both looked away, though when Terry glanced at her again, she noticed that Madeline was smiling. Terry was about to move away when Madeline spoke.

"I always enjoy coming here," she said softly, almost to herself. "The water, the sound of the waves, it always calms me down."

Terry looked around to be sure that Madeline wasn't talking to anyone else then said, "Were you upset about something?"

Madeline raised her head and looked toward Governors Island and said, "Nothing important."

The wind swept through Madeline's hair and Terry found she could not pull her eyes away. What was it? Terry thought, her profile, her expression?

Terry tried but could not remember most of what they talked about that afternoon, though they talked for several hours. Madeline mentioned that she enjoyed revival houses and Terry, who liked old musicals and dramas, suggested they see a film together sometime. She did not remember giving Madeline her phone number and was surprised when Madeline called her a day later to take Terry up on the invitation.

They saw The Ruling Class at the Film Forum and afterwards returned to Terry's apartment where Madeline insisted on making dinner. While they were eating, Madeline mentioned how she used to cook for "Jackie."

"Who's Jackie?" Terry asked.

Madeline shook her head then replied, "Old boyfriend. Well I've known him most of my life, but it wasn't until college that we decided we were in love."

Madeline went on to describe her relationship with Jack Oberon and how, in their last year of college they had planned to marry and moved in together.

"What did you study in college?" Terry asked.

"French," Madeline answered, "same as Jackie. I had illusions of moving to Paris and living like a bohemian."

"What stopped you?"

Madeline shook her head and prodded her food with a fork, saying, "Couldn't find the time."

"So, what do you do with a French major?" Terry went on.

"Jackie got a job with the U.N.," Madeline replied. "I decided on office work. Glamorous, eh?"

Terry shrugged and they both laughed.

"What happened with you two?" Terry said.

"A lot of things," Madeline replied, staring at the table. "I don't know. I loved him — once. But something was missing, you know?" She pushed herself away from the table and folded her arms in front of her, saying, "Something was missing."

"You don't have to talk about it," Terry said.

"Oh, it's nothing mysterious," Madeline said, "usual story — distance, tension, infidelity."

Saying the last word, she looked at Terry, as though trying to gauge her reaction.

Terry looked down and said almost under her breath, "Bastard."

Madeline laughed.

"No," she said, "not him."

Terry looked at her in amazement, and said, "You slept with another man?"

Madeline looked her in the eye and said emphatically, "No."

As dinner progressed, Terry found herself opening up to Madeline more and more, and was pleased to notice that Madeline seemed interested in her as well. Then, just before dinner ended, Madeline moved her hand across the table, took Terry's and said, "I hope I'm not wrong, but I don't want to leave."

"I don't want you to," Terry told her.

Terry brushed her hand across her face wiping away the tears then slowed her pace and thought *the beginning*.

She remembered their first night together, how they made love then lay in bed, holding each other all night. Who could have known it would only last two years?

She shook her head then said softly, "Two years."

Stop this. Terry held her hand against her forehead. *I'm not going through this again*.

She thought about Jack. As much as Madeline spoke of him, Terry never had any doubts of her feelings toward him. Without ever setting eyes on Jack, or even speaking to him, Terry felt an anger toward him she could not put into words, especially to Madeline, who, when talking about Jack, always did so with a voice softer than normal and a slight smile. Despite all the problems Madeline had in her relationship with Jack she was never angry toward him, nor had any harsh words for him and the more reluctant Madeline seemed to criticize Jack the more Terry despised him.

Then one night, while Madeline was at a cooking class, Terry answered the door to be met by a tall, thin, sandy-haired man with slumped shoulders and unkempt hair that was a bit too long at the sides and back. He had on a slate blue double-breasted suit with a paisley tie and round tortoise shell glasses that slid constantly down his nose, which he pushed up by applying equal pressure to each side with his thumb and middle finger. His voice was carefully measured and soft enough to cause Terry to lean slightly toward him as he said, "Does Maddie Cameron live here?"

Terry noted how different this voice sounded than the one that met her a year and a half later, enraged as it spit out the words, "I want my boy."

The first time Jack came by, Terry had not been prepared for him and before she had time to recover, he had stepped past her into the apartment and was surveying the many ceramic miniatures and decorative mugs that Madeline had brought with her when she moved in, and saying, "Obviously I've come to the right place."

"I know who you are," Terry said, pointing at him. It was all she could think to say.

"I'm sure you do," Jack replied, "Maddie here?"

"No."

Jack looked at her from over the top of his glasses then pushed them up and shook his finger at her as he said, "And I'll bet you don't want to tell me where she is."

Terry went to the farthest end of the couch from him and sat.

"What do you want, Jack?"

"I'm sorry," he proclaimed, clasping his hands in front of him and leaning forward, "you have me at a disadvantage Miss?"

"Ramsey. Terry," she said, once again feeling like a grade-schooler facing the Mother Superior.

Jack looked skyward, as though considering something then said, "Is that a nickname?"

"Look, what do you want?" Terry said.

Jack rocked back and forth on his feet and said, "I'm here to see Maddie."

"I told you," Terry said, looking away from him, "she's not here."

"Then I'll wait."

"She doesn't need you," Terry said, standing.

"I do not intend to discuss this with you," Jack said, removing his glasses and wiping them with his handkerchief then pushing them back onto his face. He regarded Terry icily.

"Dammit, what makes you think you can just come in here and pick up like nothing happened?" she said standing. "It's not you and Maddie anymore."

"You're in love with her, aren't you?" Jack said, suddenly softening his tone.

Terry looked away from him then nodded. When she looked at him again, he was rubbing his cheek with his thumb and studying the carpet. Before she could say anything, he started toward the door.

"Just tell her I came by," he said then left.

Terry gritted her teeth at the thought of Jack, and for a brief moment, felt a twinge on the right side of her face, and she touched the half-inch scar that remained under her eye. Though she tried to stop the memory, the feeling reminded her of the night three months before in the West Village when she and Madeline found themselves surrounded by the gang, none of whom could have been more than teenagers. Beyond that, Terry could tell nothing more about them, for she had not seen them.

She and Madeline had just seen a movie and were on their way back to the apartment. Madeline put her arm around Terry and set her head on Terry's shoulder — something neither of them did often while out. They were only a few blocks from the theater when Terry heard the sound of running feet, but before either she or Madeline could react, the gang was on them. One pushed Terry against a wall, holding his forearm against her shoulders, just below her neck, to prevent her from moving. She tried to push away from the wall, but the boy grabbed her hair and pulled her head back, dragging the side of her face against the building, saying, "Fuckin' dyke."

She could hear Madeline screaming "No, no" over and over and one of the boys saying in a shaky voice, "Come on, hurry, hurry."

Terry could only imagine what was happening to Madeline, thinking the worst, until, as suddenly as the attackers had come upon them, Madeline stopped screaming then all activity stopped and the boy who had been hurrying the others said, "Shit, man, what you do that for?"

And then they were gone.

Terry felt her knees go weak, just as they had in the moments after the attackers had gone and she turned to see Madeline lying on the sidewalk, her arms folded over her stomach and her knees bent slightly. Terry stepped toward her then her knees buckled, and she fell and crawled to Madeline. All she could see was the dark pool forming at Madeline's side.

"God — no, god," she said, touching Madeline's face then reaching for Madeline's stomach, but stopping short and repeating, "No."

When Terry told Madeline about Jack's visit, Madeline sat on the couch, her hands folded in front of her, and did not face Terry, who went through an extended tirade, about how Jack had burst in and refused to leave, and how, ultimately, he seemed much worse than Madeline had described him. In the long run, she concluded, it was best that Madeline had broken off the relationship. The question Terry forgot to ask at the time, but which came to dominate her thoughts in the weeks after Jack's visit, was how Jack had found Madeline in the first place. Madeline usually avoided the subject altogether and when Terry asked her directly, she shrugged, and said, "Maybe he asked around."

Still, besides the times Terry herself mentioned him, she heard little of Jack after the visit. Madeline became completely silent on the subject, a dramatic change from before when she would bring him up constantly. Other than that, their relationship changed little. They spent their afternoons filling each other in on how the day had gone, usually while lying together on the couch. They still made their monthly trips to the revival houses whenever a Renoir festival came around. Terry indulged Madeline's love for French films, even though she found them hard to follow. Each payday saw a new addition to Madeline's knickknack collection — since moving in, she'd been concentrating on Disney miniatures. Before long, Terry realized that the apartment, which had only been scantily furnished when she was there alone, was becoming over-run with Madeline's things.

But Terry said nothing about it, because she was glad to have Madeline with her. Prior to Madeline, Terry's last relationship had been five years earlier, and had ended badly, when her lover, a doctor, had transferred to a hospital on the West Coast. Meeting Madeline had filled a part of Terry's life that she had neglected ever since. Madeline was not quite ten years younger than Terry and her outlook on life was often much cheerier.

It was her singing, however, that endeared Madeline most to Terry. Whenever Madeline was cooking or working around the apartment, she'd start humming, and this would develop into a whispered song which would become louder as she went on, and Terry could not help joining in. Mornings would find the two of them engaging in duets as they hurried about preparing for work.

Terry heard the refrain, "Golden slumbers fill your eyes," and she started humming it to herself as she remembered it as a favorite of Madeline's. It was the song Madeline was singing the time Terry came in and found her joyfully bouncing around the kitchen. When she noticed Terry, she ran to her and threw her arms around her then sang to her for a moment, before taking Terry's hands and saying, "Come here, I've got some wonderful news."

And Terry sat on the couch and looked into Madeline's eyes and listened to what she said, but something wasn't right, so Terry said, "What?"

"I'm pregnant," Madeline repeated.

Terry stared blankly at her for several minutes then yelled, "Pregnant? How can you be pregnant?"

"I don't know," Madeline said, sliding away from her, and folding her hands in her lap, "the usual way I guess."

"You know what I mean," Terry said. She stood and threw her hands up and said, "You were with Jack, weren't you?"

"Well, he came by to talk, and —"

"You did it here, in our apartment?"

Terry turned away from Madeline. Madeline stood and went to her then rubbed Terry's shoulders and said, "Come on. Let's talk about this, okay."

Terry did not respond.

"It doesn't mean anything," Madeline went on. "Can't you understand?"

"What am I supposed to understand?" Terry said.

"I care about Jack. Not like I do you, but just as strongly. You and I can still be together, though. That doesn't have to change."

"It's already changed."

"No," Madeline said, putting her arms around Terry. "I still feel the same. I really do."

Terry had remained with Madeline, though she no longer trusted her. Jack started spending more time at the apartment, usually stopping in once or twice a week. Whenever one of his visits was scheduled, Terry made sure she had a class or film to attend so as not to be around him.

Terry had no idea what Madeline and Jack did while she was out, though once Terry came in and found that Jack was still there. He was sitting on the arm of the couch, slumped over, resting his elbows on his knees, his head on his hands. Madeline was seated at the middle of the couch, leaning back, arms crossed. They were watching television.

"It was just that one time," Madeline explained when Terry asked about her and Jack. "We only did it once after we broke up — I just got pregnant."

After Joey was born Jack livened up considerably. His visits were highlighted by stuffed animals and baby blankets and clothing, and he was always anxious to engage Terry in a discussion of the latest child development book he'd read.

"The first years are the most important," he'd say, rubbing his hands together. "I'm going to make sure I do everything right."

Then he'd launch into a flurry of quotes from Dr. Spock, or

some other published expert. Though she never admitted it to Jack or Madeline, Terry had also started reading baby books and quizzing people at work who had children. Terry spent more time at the apartment, even when Jack was around, looking for any opportunity to hold Joey, or bathe him, and she began to match Jack in buying presents.

The one who made it all worthwhile was Joey himself. When Madeline brought him home Terry had avoided any contact with him, fearing she might drop him, or give him some exotic disease she'd picked up on the subway. Madeline finally convinced Terry to take him. She showed Terry how to hold him then placed a towel over Terry's shoulder and before Terry had time to protest, she had him cradled in her arms.

Terry was very stiff at first and made hardly any movements with him, fearing she would trip over something, but as she took him more, she gained confidence, and was soon dancing around the apartment, spinning with him and making faces, which, as Joey grew older, made him laugh wildly.

From the start, Terry recognized Madeline in Joey's face. They shared the same eyes and dark hair, and though Madeline always protested that Joey took after his father, each time Terry looked at Joey, it was Madeline who greeted her. Sometimes, Madeline would bring Joey into the bed with them and he would lie between them fast asleep. Then Madeline would talk of how things would be when Joey grew up and of how the three of them would be like a family. Terry saw Joey, asleep on the bed, Madeline, also asleep, beside him.

God-dammit Jack, you can't do this.

"He's my son," Jack said the first time he came by to take Joey. "Regardless of what you think of me that's the fact. Now, where is he?"

"You never cared about Maddie. All she ever was for you was a—"

"Come on, I know she must have talked about me to you."

Terry, turning red, yelled, "I want you out of here now."

"Not without my son," he said, moving further into the apartment.

"I said get out."

"Where is he?" he said, grabbing her roughly by the arms and shaking her. "I want my boy."

"What are you going to do," Terry said. "Beat me up?"

He released her.

"Is that what you think I'm capable of?" he said, moving quickly away from her.

"I don't know what you're capable of," Terry said.

"What did Maddie say? She knew what I was capable of. What did she tell you?"

She looked at Jack and, noting his expression, said, "Yeah, she talked about you. Sometimes all she talked about was you."

Jack nodded.

"And you know," Terry went on, "I think she could have gone back to you. I was always afraid she would."

"You don't have a clue," Jack blurted out then lowered his head.

Terry stared at him for several minutes then said, "You knew — even back then?"

Jack nodded.

"The first time," he said, "she told me it was curiosity, just to see what it was like. What was I supposed to say to her? I don't know anything about that sort of thing. Besides, she moved in with me, so I dismissed it." He pressed his hands against the wall then turned and said, "The next ones she kept from me — tried to at least. But I knew."

"If you knew then why —"

"Did I stay with her?" he said. He shrugged then said, "What she said. How she acted. Even though I knew she was with other women she never acted any differently towards me. It was almost as though there was no one else."

The words touched something in Terry, and she realized it had been much the same between her and Madeline, even though Jack had returned. Terry looked at Jack, who now stood before her, shaking his head slowly. She went to him and, touching his arm, said, "Why can't you just stop this, Jack? You don't have time for Joey. Leave him with me. Please."

"Leave him with you," Jack said harshly. "That would solve everything wouldn't it?" He went to the door but stopped before going out and said, "What would you do? Answer that, okay? If the situation were reversed, what would you do?"

Two days later the summons arrived.

As she continued up Broadway, Terry withdrew the summons from her coat pocket. Looking at it she said through clenched teeth, "Bastard." She started to rip it in half then checked herself, thinking, Nothing I can do. Nothing I can do.

"I'm afraid there's nothing you can do, Miss Ramsey," she heard the legal aid lawyer say. "You're not the boy's mother."

"Me and Maddie are the only family he's ever had," Terry said. "Jack has no right to take him away."

"The courts don't see it that way," the lawyer said.

"I am more of a parent to Joey than Jack ever was."

"Maybe so. Unfortunately you have no biological ties to him."

No biological ties, she thought. *Is that all these bastards care about? I'm as good as his parent. I've earned that. Where was Jack when Maddie was in labor for twenty hours? Where was Jack period?*

After Madeline died, Jack made the funeral arrangements, a graveside service attended only by him and Terry.

"Her parents are dead," he explained.

At one point, just as the priest finished speaking, Terry began to sob quietly, and Jack put his hand on her back. She leaned against him and was glad that he was there, that she didn't have to say good-bye to Madeline by herself.

Afterwards, they went back to his rented car but did not get in. They just stood, alternately looking then not looking at one another.

"Well," Jack said then cleared his throat and clasped his hands in front of him.

"I can't believe it," Terry started, but couldn't finish.

"I know," Jack said. He looked at her then leaned his head to one side and lightly ran his finger over the bandage on Terry's face, saying, "How are you getting along?"

"Doctor said I'll be good as new in a few weeks," she replied. She paused then said, "What does he know?"

Jack nodded. He drove her back to the apartment and saw her to the door. Terry stepped inside then looked at Jack and stepped out again and hugged him.

"Thanks," she said.

"Sure."

She started to close the door, but Jack halted her.

"Oh, before I forget, I'm going out of town for a few days," he said. "I'll come pick up Joey when I get back."

"What do you mean?"

"He's my son," Jack said. "He's going to come live with me."

"Oh, no. No, you don't. Maddie wanted me to take care of him."

Jack stared at her for several minutes then said, "Let's not start this, okay. I know what Maddie wanted."

"Do you? Did she tell you?"

"She didn't have to. I knew her. I've known her all her life. We thought the same way."

Terry bowed her head, saying, "I can't go into this right now. Dammit, Jack, you don't understand."

"No, I don't. And obviously you don't either." He moved away from the door, saying, "We'll talk about it when I get back."

Yeah, we talked all right. But what good did it do?

Terry stopped when she came within view of her building, realizing she could not go in, could not hand Joey over to Jack. She went to a phone booth a block away and hastily dialed the apartment.

"Mrs. Wilson?" she said when the babysitter answered. She hesitated then said, "Joey's father — you remember Jack, don't you? Yeah, that's him." She paused briefly then her voice cracked when she said, "Well," so she stopped and cleared her throat and went on, "Jack's coming by in a little while and he's picking Joey up and — and could you get Joey's things together?" Terry looked toward the building again and said, "No — no, I don't think I'll make it back by then. Just tell Jack —" Terry paused for several seconds then finished, "No, never mind."

She hung up and slowly started away from her building. She had gone two and a half blocks before she knew where she had to go and picked up her pace. She headed down Broadway, past Canal, past the lawyer's office near city hall and through the financial center until she at last found herself at the harbor. Once there, she quickly moved to the railing and leaned on it then lowered her head and closed her eyes. She had no idea how long she stood there but she was determined to remain. She heard a clink on the railing nearby and opened her eyes expecting to see someone standing there.

She was alone.

Terry turned and leaned back against the railing and discovered that there was no one even within sight. A chilling wind blew past her, but Terry did not sense the cold. Instead she sighed and looked skyward then thought, *So, this is how it ends.*

A Bad Day's Work

"Tell me, Mr. Willoughby" — Jason looked across the massive, nearly empty desk that belonged to Dave Summers of Ads Unlimited — "what sort of experience do you have that would qualify you to be editor of The Flagship?"

His interview with Summers was Jason's fifth in three weeks, and as he considered his answer, he did so with the sinking feeling that this one would go as well as the previous ones.

Jason was twenty, but his face, sans the moustache he usually wore, made him look much younger. His eyes betrayed the fact that he'd not been sleeping well. His hair had been combed at one time, but the wind outside, combined with Jason's habit of constantly raking his fingers through his hair had mussed it. Jason sat nervously in the chair, leaning forward, his elbows resting on his knees, his right thumb flopping back and forth, bouncing up and down, as though he was playing an imaginary drum.

"Well—" Jason shifted nervously in his chair, and then adjusted his tie, "I type 40 words a minute, and I've had some experience on a newspaper."

"What sort of experience?"

Summers smiled and Jason could see his teeth, perfectly straight and white. Everything about Summers looked phony, blond hair permanently groomed, as though Summers had never been out in the wind and a blue pin-striped suit so straight it looked like it probably had looked in the window at Brooks Brothers.

"Well, uh, I was on the newspaper staff in high school," Jason said, adjusting his tie again, "and I've worked with my company's newsletter — writing articles, mainly. The job of editor shouldn't be much of a problem, though."

"What about college?"

"I — well — I haven't gone. Not yet. I do plan to, though."

Summers wrote something on his notepad.

"I see by your application that your current job with — ah, Douglas Frazier — by the way, what does a customs broker do?"

"We work for companies bringing goods into the U.S. — getting them cleared through U.S. customs and delivered."

"I see," Summers said, raising his eyebrows mechanically. "Why do you want to leave your current job?"

"I don't think I'm making enough money," Jason said. "I

know I'm not, that is." Jason coughed then cleared his throat and tugged at his tie, "And I'd like to, uh, find something closer to my career objective."

"What might that be?"

"Writing — I'm a writer."

Summers wrote something more on his pad then looked over what he had written as though he was a kindergartner admiring his first drawing.

"Frankly, Mr. Willoughby, you don't have much to offer us."

Jason leaned forward in the chair and grabbed the edge of Summers' desk.

"Look," he said, "I can do a good job if you'll only—"

"Mr. Willoughby, please," Summers said, looking around quickly, though there was no one else in the office, "I'm not judging you. It's just that you lack the skills we require."

Jason fell back in the chair and said, "I see."

He tapped his leg nervously.

"Now, if you were more experienced, or could show us some of your published work, things might be different."

Jason stood and said, "Thanks for seeing me."

He walked out, ignoring Summers, who gave his practiced line, "Good luck in your future endeavors."

Jason put on his overcoat then caught a bus headed down-town. It was crowded, and Jason was pressed in between a Hispanic woman holding onto a little boy, and a Hassidic Jewish man reading a paper. Each time the bus stopped or started Jason bumped into one or the other and almost immediately after he had gotten on, the little boy began staring at him. Jason looked down at him then away then back again. He tried to turn, so that he was facing in a different direction, but the bus was too crowded, and he couldn't move. Finally, he focused over the boy's head at a woman who'd gotten on a few stops back. Jason pinned his eyes on her then, when she looked up and caught him, he gave her a bit of a smile. She looked down then back up and finding him still looking, said, "What?"

Jason dropped his eyes, only to be met by the continual stare of the boy. He left the bus three blocks from his office and walked the rest of the way.

As Jason was hanging up his coat, Mr. Bugg, his supervisor, approached him. Bugg was a short, paunchy man, with dark, graying hair, that was thinning in front. He had the same, grey, striped tie with the small patch of dried egg on it, which he kept, already tied, in his office and slipped on each morning when he got in. Bugg's wire-framed glasses had broken and were held together by a bent paper clip.

"Glad you could join us, Willoughby," Bugg said intensely, but in a low voice. "Trouble on the subway?"

"I was at the doctor," Jason said.

"Oh, sick again?" Bugg said. "Why is it I never see any insurance forms? I want a note next time."

"Sure," Jason said then went to his desk.

It had been nearly a year since Jason answered the ad in the Village Voice and had first introduced himself to Mr. Bugg. The ad said Douglas Frazier was looking for a courier and promised good wages and an opportunity to advance. Jason had received both, though in one year's time his good wages had gone from adequate to hardly enough and his opportunity for advancement had led him into a boring job he wasn't really qualified to do. He had gone from being a courier, who spent most of his time outside the office shuttling papers, to a clerk, confined to a desk all day.

"You know how to add don't you?" Mr. Bugg said when Jason voiced his initial reservations about the promotion. "You can type."

"Well, yes," Jason replied.

"Then the job will be a snap," Bugg said. "That's all you do, add a few numbers here and there and type a little."

In his new job Jason mainly typed "entries," which described for customs officials the sort of merchandise being brought into the country, its value and the importers name. Jason had taken typing in school, but never counted his keyboard skills among his assets. His duties also included ordering supplies for the office, and it was here that he usually ran afoul of Mr. Bugg.

Jason's phone buzzed and he looked at it then at Frank, whose desk was across from his. Frank shrugged, and Jason picked up the phone.

"Willoughby!" Bugg's voice assaulted his ear. "My office."

Jason rose and passed Frank, who shook his finger at Jason.

Bugg was on the phone when Jason walked in and motioned for Jason to sit. He did and looked over the cluttered desk that was piled high with files. On one end, Jason noticed a framed picture of Bugg, his wife and two daughters that lay on its back, partially covered with files.

"Willoughby, Willoughby, Willoughby," Bugg said, hanging up the phone and grabbing a handful of bills. "Let me introduce you to a new concept, okay?" He shoved the bills at Jason and said, "We can't spend more than we take in. Look at those bills — how do you explain those purchases?"

"We need supplies," Jason said, glancing at the bills without picking them up. "How are we supposed to get along without them?"

"Look at the prices!" Bugg said, just under a yell. "Nobody pays $50 for a case of Xerox paper. Do you make an effort to find the most expensive items you can?"

Jason shrugged and said, "Company's turning a profit isn't it?"

"That's not the point," Bugg said quickly. He stopped and put his hands up and took a deep breath then leaned forward. "Willoughby, you've been here what, almost a year?"

Jason nodded.

"Not quite a year," Bugg said. "See, you were doing pretty well at what you were hired for, so, I decided to give you a shot at something a little more challenging, you know?"

Again, Jason nodded.

"But when I gave you authority to make purchases over my signature, that was not an invitation to go out and have a spending spree," Bugg said, his voice rising with each word. "Am I making sense? Do you get my meaning?"

"Sure," Jason said. He thought about the forty cases of typewriter ribbon a phone solicitor had badgered Jason into ordering two days earlier but decided not to mention them.

Mr. Bugg leaned back and relaxed a bit then said, "Level with me, Willoughby. You don't really like working here, do you?"

"I can live with it," Jason said, tugging at his tie.

"No, really, you don't like it, eh?"

"It has its ups and downs," Jason replied. "I can live with it."

Bugg covered his face and shook his head. Then, exasperated, he said, "Don't buy anything else, okay? From here on out, I'll handle all purchases."

"Sure thing," Jason said, rising quickly.

He went back into the main office and over to the coffee machine, where Frank was getting a cup. Jason shook his head and rolled his eyes as he approached.

Frank wasn't like Jason. An account executive, Frank actually met with clients, and had oversight on the accounts Jason worked. Frank was in his last year of college, athletic and energetic and obsessed with status and promotion.

"You know Barry in exports has been here twice as long as I have," Frank once told Jason, "but I'm already making $5000 more a year than he is."

"How'd you manage that?" Jason asked, disinterested.

"Ambition, my boy," Frank told him. "All you need is a little drive, that's all." Frank eyed Jason's clothing and said, "This stuff you wear, it won't get you anyplace."

"What's wrong with my clothes?" Jason asked.

Frank checked off on his hands as he said, "Striped shirt, no jacket, corduroys, mismatched tie — and tennis shoes? What's right with that look?"

Frank never had to worry about the impression he made. He was tall and dark-haired and had what could be called a winning smile, and he always overdressed for any occasion. His suits came in only two colors, navy and dark grey, and his shirts, were usually little more than tinted a certain shade, and rarely stood out. The only ornament he ever allowed himself was an occasional striped or polka-dotted tie.

"What'd Bugg want?" Frank said.

"Purchases," Jason said, "he acts like we're going out of business."

"Hey, every time he saves some money, he gets a little bonus in his paycheck. Didn't you know that?"

Bugg walked by, and seeing Frank and Jason there, said, "Coffee break's over, ladies."

Frank returned to his desk, and Jason poured a cup of coffee. He went back to his desk, but could not concentrate, so he went into the bathroom and splashed his face with cold water and tried to wake up.

Jason was from Atlanta and had been in New York for a year and a half. He had applied to City University and was accepted, though once he got to New York, he postponed his plans indefinitely. He spent the first six months using up most of the money he had saved during high school then began in earnest looking for a job.

The courier's position sounded good from the start for two reasons: First, it required no skill; and second, it would give him a chance to walk around and see the city while getting paid and he had made the most of this opportunity from the start, usually adding about twenty or thirty minutes to estimates of the time it would take him to get to and from various locations. He learned, almost the first week that all he needed to say was, "Trouble on the subway," and he could get away with taking an hour and a half to travel from the office on 23rd Street to Whitehall Street where Customs was located and back. He almost never had to show up at the office at all, except to pick up papers and receive delivery instructions. Jason did such a good job as the courier that Bugg dubbed him "Mr. Speedy," and raised his salary twice in the first six months he worked there.

Then Jason was promoted. This really wasn't Jason's fault, for he had never acted in a manner that suggested he wanted to be promoted — just bad timing on his part. Jason had been there for just over six months when several clerks quit at once, leaving a big gap in an already overworked staff. New applications were scarce, so as a last-ditch effort, Jason found himself cajoled by Mr. Bugg into accepting the new position. A new person was hired to do his old job. He was given a quick overview of what his duties would include, given about a week of instruction in preparing entries then Bugg assigned him twelve accounts.

That was the high point.

Jason turned his attention to the clock and watched the slow-motion progression of the hour hand as it crept toward lunch time. Then, as he was standing to go, Chris, the office manager, came over with a pad and said, "What'll you have, Jason?"

Jason looked at her and noted her creamy skin and auburn hair and noticed how the silk fabric of her blouse glided over her breasts, outlining them. He smiled and said, "That's all right, I'm going out for lunch."

"No, you're not," Chris said authoritatively. "Mr. Bugg told me to tell you that you took today's lunch yesterday when you were gone for two and a half hours."

Grinding his teeth together, he fell back into the chair.

"Get me a ham on rye," he snapped. "And tell them not to put mustard on this one."

"Yes sir," Chris said sarcastically. She started away.

"Make sure you say, `No mustard.'"

"I heard you the first time," she said.

"Underline it," Jason said without looking at her.

She rolled her eyes and walked away. Jason leaned back and

drummed his fingers on the desk top. He rubbed his temples then picked up his coffee cup and found it empty. While he was at the coffee machine, Mr. Bugg walked by and, seeing him, stopped.

"Willoughby, why is it every time I come out here, you're away from your desk?"

"Bad timing, I guess," Jason said shrugging.

Bugg shook his head and walked away.

When Jason interviewed for his job at Douglas Frazier, at least seven phone calls came in which Bugg accepted and dispatched within moments. Jason noted that almost every phrase Bugg said set off an association in his mind and he made notes of "things to remember to do." The interview consisted of hardly more than Bugg asking Jason, "You like to walk around a lot?"

"Sure," Jason said, shrugging.

The phone rang again and Bugg snatched it up and began what promised to be a long conversation.

"Hold it a minute," he said to the other party. He looked at Jason, and said, "You able to start this Monday?"

Jason started Monday.

While he was working out of the office and only checking in sporadically, Jason thought of Mr. Bugg as a little uptight, but not out of the ordinary. It wasn't until Jason was promoted and exposed to Bugg on a daily basis that he began to be annoyed by Bugg, who's management style was to have no definable style. There was never any way to predict how Bugg would react to a situation. Sometimes, when Jason decided to leave an account until the next morning, Bugg would get hysterical, claiming that Jason's decision could "cost the company millions, millions!" Then other times, when Jason reluctantly mentioned he might not be able to finish a file by closing time, Bugg would clap him on the shoulder, laugh and say, "It can wait."

At meetings, called weekly, Bugg never singled anyone out for criticism. Regardless of who was causing problems, Bugg gave his usual, "We all need to work much harder," speech, before launching into a litany of areas where improvement was needed, and he had mentioned the same areas so many times, that Jason could recite them by heart. Should anyone approach Bugg with a specific complaint about another employee, Bugg's answer was to call a "special" meeting and berate everyone for not carrying an equal share of the work load.

Chris passed Jason's desk and dropped the bag with his sandwich onto it and walked away without a word. Jason opened it to find the sandwich buried under handfuls of mustard packets. He fished out the sandwich, and threw the bag away.

Frank returned from lunch but before he could take his seat, Jason motioned him over. Frank sat on the edge of Jason's desk and said, "What now?"

"I need some advice," Jason said. Pointing, he added, "No sarcasm, okay?"

Frank shrugged.

"What if you weren't happy with your job?" Jason began.

"I'd quit," Frank said, cutting him off. "Anything else?"

"Hold on, will you?" Jason said. "What if you didn't have any other options?"

Frank stood and knocked on Jason's desk as he said, "About the only thing I've learned in three and a half years at N.Y.U. — there are always options."

Jason rubbed his eyes and shook his head then replied, "But what if you had rent and bills and other things to pay for? How could you —"

Frank held up his hand to stop Jason then leaned close to him and said in a strong whisper, "Look, if you don't like it here, quit. If, for some bizarre masochistic reason you enjoy it here, then stay. But whatever you decide, leave me out of it. I'm tired of hearing you whine about it."

"But Frank —"

"No buts," Frank said, straightening. "I've had enough." He turned to go then stopped, turned back and said, "Have you ever thought that if you were unemployed you might have more incentive to find something better?"

"Unemployment is what got me into this mess," Jason said.

"Enough!" Frank said, returning to his desk.

Jason sighed and tapped his desk with a pencil then looked at the door to Bugg's office. He shook his head and rubbed his eyes again and said, "I can't."

He closed the file he'd been working on then thumbed through a pile Bugg had given him before lunch to find one that seemed more interesting. Sandwiched between two files, was a single sheet of paper which Jason removed and looked over. At the top, in large bold letters, were the words, "Mandatory Personnel Reductions." The body of the memo stated that employees needed to be laid off and supervisors with stars beside their names had yet to make necessary cuts. Bugg's name had four stars.

Jason placed the memo atop the file he was working on and took it to Frank.

"Check this out," Jason said.

Frank read the memo and shook his head, saying, "That man can't make a decision to save his life."

"This would help, wouldn't it?" Jason said. "I mean, if Bugg cut me then —"

"Then you could apply for unemployment, and it would look better than if you were fired," Frank said. "I mean, nobody has any control over lay-offs."

"Yeah," Jason said. "I'll go talk to Bugg."

Frank grabbed Jason's arm and said, "No, you idiot. You don't ask someone to lay you off. That's the same as quitting." He released Jason then Frank propped his head on his hand. "Let me think about this." He paused then snapped his fingers. "Jason, my boy, there just might be a way I can help you."

Frank sent Jason back to his desk with instructions to "Stand by."

Jason remained at his desk for an hour, constantly looking up to see what Frank was doing. Frank never looked up but continued working on the file on his desk and Jason finally stopped waiting and devoted his full attention once more to the files on his desk.

Suddenly, Frank slammed his hand onto his desk and yelled, "That's it!"

Jason looked up quickly to see Frank glaring at him.

"What is it?" Jason said.

Frank grabbed the file off his desk and headed toward Jason, saying "I'm fed up with your incompetence. You make me — hell, you make the whole company look bad with your ridiculous mistakes."

Frank was in front of Jason's desk, waving the file around as he spoke. The whole office ceased activity and formed a loose semi-circle around Jason and Frank. Mr. Bugg came out of his office and said, "What's all the commotion?"

"I've had enough of this idiot's bungling," Frank said, pointing at Jason. "He's going to screw up big one day and cost us a ton of money. I'm not going to put up with it anymore."

"Now Frank, just calm down," Bugg said, moving to the desk. "I'm sure we can work this out."

"There's nothing to work out," Frank said. He paused and looked around to be sure he had everyone's attention then proclaimed, "Either Jason goes, or I do."

A low rumble went through the crowd and Frank crossed his arms to indicate he was finished.

Mr. Bugg lowered his head and removed his glasses then ran his hand over his brow.

"I'm sorry you feel that way, Frank," he said as he replaced his glasses. "But it just isn't that simple."

Frank and Jason together said, "What?"

"No Jason, you stay out of this," Bugg said. "Frank I'm sure we can work something out, but there's no reason to be so absolute about all this."

"You don't understand," Frank said. "I'm not negotiating — I'm dead serious. Now make your decision."

Bugg shook his head and laughed weakly then said, "Take a break, Frank. Get you some coffee and calm down a little. Then I can talk to you both and maybe —"

"Talk to us both?" Frank exclaimed. "Talk to us both?" He grabbed Bugg by the shoulders and shook him, saying, "Can't you make a decision on anything, you imbecile? Can't you take any responsibility, you gutless—"

Bugg pulled away from Frank and straightened his clothing, all the while glaring at Frank.

"I — I cannot tolerate this at all," Bugg said, "not at all." He hesitated then pushed his glasses up and said, "I'm sorry Frank, but I'll have to let you go."

"What?" Jason cried. "You can't —"

Frank held up his hand to silence Jason.

"It'll be my pleasure," Frank said to Bugg. Frank went to his desk and grabbed his jacket then entered Bugg's office slamming the door. Jason watched as Frank and Bugg, both standing, argued behind the door then Bugg bent down and wrote something on a piece of paper and handed it to Frank. After this, Frank walked out. Jason caught him halfway to the door.

"Don't do this," Jason said. "Let me go see Bugg. I'll quit, I swear —"

"Listen," Frank said, "it's not you this time, okay? I know what I said earlier, but once I got into it, I realized I needed to do this."

"But Frank —"

"I'm sorry things didn't work out," Frank said. "I really am."

He started past Jason then said, "It's easy, okay? Just walk in and do it. It doesn't hurt."

Frank collected his overcoat and was gone.

Jason looked after him for a moment then turned and stared at Bugg's office door. He started slowly toward the door, but as he moved, he picked up speed until he was moving in a furious march. He entered Bugg's office and closed the door then crossed his arms as he looked down at Mr. Bugg, who was seated and wiping his forehead with a handkerchief.

"Willoughby," Bugg said, looking up. "It's good you're here. We need to talk."

"We do?" Jason said, uncrossing his arms.

"Yes, we do," Bugg replied, motioning for Jason to sit. "After what just happened — well, let's just say it opened my eyes. Frank was a good man, and his loss will be felt in more ways than one."

Jason nodded and fought back a smile at what he was sure was coming next.

"But there's no reason you should be affected by it at all," Bugg said.

"What?" Jason said, leaning forward.

"I know you were probably worried about it," Bugg said. "No doubt that's what brought you in here. But let me assure you that Frank's departure will not change your status with this company."

"I don't believe this," Jason said. "Mr. Bugg, I —"

"No, no," Bugg said. "Let me finish. I had a tough decision to make today. The company's been pressing me to get rid of a worker and frankly, Willoughby, I had decided it'd be you. I was going to tell you after work. But Frank's departure made that unnecessary." Bugg paused and leaned back. "I'll be reassigning you to Barry in exports. He's not as productive as Frank, but maybe that's what you need right now." Bugg leaned forward and pointed at Jason, saying, "But be sure of this, your job at this company is safe for as long as you want it."

Jason looked at Bugg and for a moment, felt the words rising to his mouth, but then his courage waned, and he could say nothing. Slowly, he rose and headed toward the door.

"Thanks," Jason said. "That's a load off my mind."

Shocks to the System

Harry Bailey had just killed his roommate. While Frank was sitting at the kitchen table, sipping his morning coffee, Harry walked up behind him and clunked him in the head with the heavy iron frying pan that normally hung on a nail by the stove. Then, when Frank spun off the chair, falling to his knees, looked up at Harry with a dull, questioning look, and tried to gurgle out some sort of demand for an explanation, Harry reared back his arms and brought the frying pan down again with all his strength, dealing the fatal blow.

This had been an hour previous, and now Harry did not know how to proceed. The murder had occurred quickly and coldly. Harry did not think or feel a thing throughout the whole ordeal, but now, as Frank's body lay in the breakfast nook — Harry had remembered to put newspapers under Frank's head to make clean-up easier — Harry was awakening to the full realization of what he'd done and what now lay ahead of him. Harry did not regret killing Frank. There was no question in Harry's mind that it had to be done. Still it had opened up a world of new problems for Harry.

Just like always, Frank. You're dead, but you're still causing me grief.

Harry, fully dressed, was seated in his room, which lay just off the kitchen. He switched on Wheel of Fortune, hoping to clear his mind, to come up with his next move. Immediately, Vanna White filled the screen, looking particularly striking in a blue sequined mini dress with spaghetti straps. The puzzle, Harry could tell instantly, was "Prince of Wales." There were four letters showing already and the person whose turn it was bought an "a," then guessed "Prince of Walls?"

"You idiot," Harry yelled, pounding his hands against his thigh, "Prince of Walls? What the hell does that mean?"

He shut off the television, shaking his head, saying, "Why do the idiots get all the breaks?"

His face reflected back from the blank screen, a non-descript face, one easily lost in a crowd.

Not the face of a killer, he thought.

The brown, narrow, semi-circles of his eyes drooped at the edges, and had wide creases underneath and bushy dark brows above them which moved up and down in tune with his emotions. The beat-up suede loafer on his sockless right foot dangled from his toes.

He turned his eyes to the bare, lifeless legs which issued from under Frank's red and white striped housecoat. Harry sighed and rubbed his hands roughly over his eyes.

"Frankie, Frankie, Frankie," he said, "what um uh gunna do wit' jue?"

Harry stood and stepped into the kitchen to examine Frank's body, and determine, if necessary, how far he'd be able to carry him. The blood flow had stopped, though Frank still wore the dull look he had given Harry just before the final blow. His sandy colored hair was marred by a browning gash which ran along the center part. The newspapers under his head were filled with the same browning color. As was usual in the morning, Frank was clothed only in jockey shorts and the red and white robe. It was marked with ketchup and jelly stains and lighter stains Harry couldn't identify.

One of the few things Frank never insisted on being spotless.

Frank was nearly a foot taller than Harry, and thinner, though Harry was more bulky and muscular, especially in the chest and legs. Still Harry didn't relish the prospect of getting rid of Frank. Harry didn't own a car, nor did he have access to one. He'd considered, even planned the murder up to the actual killing, but had not thought himself capable of committing the deed and therefore had not determined what to do afterward. He needed to think, to determine a plan. He checked his pockets to be sure he had his keys and wallet and headed toward the front door.

"Hiya, Harry," he heard as he was locking the apartment door in the foyer. The apartment was on the bottom floor of a two-family row house. Upstairs were Bill and Angie, an unmarried couple in their mid-twenties. Harry turned to find Angie standing at the foot of the stairs, about to ascend, a shopping bag under her arm.

"Oh, hi," he said, brightening. He went to the railing and continued, "You off today?"

"Now you know I don't go in on Fridays," she replied, with a smile. An electric jolt shot through Harry's body when she smiled and his heart beat faster. Angie was pretty, with light brown hair and delicate features, clearly defined cheekbones and a thin, sharp nose. Her eyes were violet and widened whenever she was happy or excited. They widened as Harry returned her smile.

"The question is, why are you still around," she said. "You

usually leave around eight, don't you?"

Harry grinned and leaned against the railing, saying, "Checking up on me, are you?"

Angie chuckled, blushing and lowering her head. "No — it's just I know you leave right before I normally do."

"Angie!" Bill's coarse voice boomed from above. "You get my cigs?"

Angie rolled her eyes then mouthed, "Gotta go," to Harry and started up the stairs, saying, "Yeah, hon."

As she reached the top, Harry heard Bill say, "Who the hell were you talking to?"

"I was being neighborly," Angie said.

"Get in here," Bill replied, followed by a slamming door.

"Idiot," Harry said about Bill, wondering how Angie had ended up with someone like that.

Harry had not dealt with Bill very much. He usually never left the apartment before nightfall and was often out until one or two in the morning, often returning drunk. His return would be followed by loud stomping and nearly an hour's worth of verbal abuse directed toward Angie. Harry had lain in bed many nights, listening to Bill's loud, raspy voice as he insulted his girlfriend. Often Bill would drop off after his tirades and would sleep until mid-day. Sometimes Harry would see him when returning from work. Bill, his shoulder-length dark hair uncombed and his old clothes rumpled, would be chain smoking, seated on the front steps of the building, seeming like a homeless person who'd wandered into the neighborhood by mistake and was resting briefly. Bill had dull green eyes and eyebrows that met in the center of his face. His jaw jutted out, giving his face a lantern shape and he was inevitably unshaven and always seemed disoriented as Harry stepped past him approaching the door.

"Tell your roommate to mind his god-damned business," Bill would often say.

While Harry had learned to endure Bill's late-night outbursts, Frank had never been as tolerant and frequently went up to complain about the noise. Frank's concern, however, was never for Angie, the object of the outbursts, but for Frank's own missed sleep.

"She must ask for it, living with someone like that," Frank frequently remarked on the matter. "She doesn't like it, she should leave."

The problem with Frank's complaining was that it often had

the opposite effect on Bill. Following one of Frank's visits, Bill would stomp around more, running up and down the hallway, or he'd turn his stereo up really loud. This would lead to another visit from Frank and a loud shouting match and more confusion upstairs until Bill would pass out after which the apartment would fall silent.

There was a time in Harry's stay at the apartment when he was relatively satisfied with his situation. When he first moved in, he was sharing with Clark and Simone, a couple who'd lived there for several years. The apartment was what New Yorkers refer to as a railroad flat, an apartment that consisted of three connected rooms that had a designated living room, but no specific bedroom area and the way Clark and Simone marked off the apartment was to close the double doors between the back room and the small middle room, taking it and the living room and giving Harry the medium-sized back room. A short while after Harry moved in, the people upstairs moved out and Bill and Angie replaced them.

Harry met Angie long before he met Bill, when he ran into her coming and going from work. Sometimes, they'd share a subway ride if they happened to leave at the same time. They eventually established a pattern of leaving together each Tuesday and Thursday, until one morning, Harry noticed Bill watching them from the upstairs window. The following Tuesday, Harry stopped in the foyer to await Angie, but she didn't come down. After nearly five minutes, Harry went upstairs and tapped on the door.

He was met by an agitated Bill, who angrily looked him over then said, "What the hell do you want?"

"I just wanted to see if Angie was —"

"She ain't going to work," Bill said and slammed the door in Harry's face.

That afternoon, when Harry came in, Angie was waiting on the stairs.

"Hi," she said, standing as he entered. She went to him and touched his arm as she said softly, "Listen, I'm sorry about this morning, but Bill's —"

"Don't worry," Harry said. "I don't blame you."

"Thanks," she said, smiling then starting upstairs.

"Why do you put up with that crap," Harry said. "The way he

acts."

Angie spun slowly and leaned heavily on the railing with both hands.

"It's — hard to explain," she said. "I ask myself that sometime — but —"

"But what," Harry said, stepping up onto the stairs. "You're better than that."

"Look, the other guys in my life didn't stick around," she said. "Bill's the only one who's stayed." She turned and proceeded up.

"Maybe you should've waited a little longer," Harry said.

Angie turned at the top step and looked down at Harry then let out a brief laugh and said, "Maybe."

After that, he only saw Angie occasionally.

He had more to worry about anyway, after he came in one afternoon to find Clark and Simone waiting for him in the kitchen.

"We've found a new place," Clark said, "this great condo in Manhattan. So —"

Their plan was to move mid-April; it was March 31.

Harry was not normally very sociable, and did not know many people. After nearly two weeks of searching for a new roommate, he was ready to begin looking for a new place, when some people at work introduced him to Frank, who was being ousted from his place which was going condo. Two visits from Frank to look at the apartment, and a week's worth of worrying on Harry's part passed before Frank agreed to move in.

There was, however, half a month between Clark and Simone's departure and Frank's arrival and in the meantime, Harry took full advantage of his privacy. He immediately claimed the small middle room, taking over half the apartment and he set about switching the utility bills over to his name, which gave him an overwhelming sense of responsibility, which he enjoyed. Harry had lived with his parents throughout college and a few years afterwards - longer than he should have, he felt - so this, his first real taste of living on his own was particularly satisfying. At last, he felt he was making progress.

Frank moved in one afternoon while Harry was at work, so that when he returned home, Frank was just completing his unpacking. In a way, Harry had been disappointed he had not been able to afford the whole rent on the apartment, because he had liked the idea of having a separate living room, in case he ever had anyone over. But having Frank there took away the burden of paying $800 a month, and for a while, Harry was glad to have him around. Both had bachelor's degrees in similar fields — Harry's English, Frank's Journalism — and both were working on advanced degrees. What Harry liked most about Frank, was that he didn't go out of his way to hang around with Harry, who liked his privacy. If he and Frank ran into each other in the kitchen, which they shared, they'd exchange a few words, or maybe have a brief conversation, but if Harry was in his room, Frank almost never interrupted him, and Harry extended the same courtesy.

There was, however, a distance between them, a coldness that Harry was always conscious of, but never understood. At times, when he and Frank would pass in the kitchen and Harry would say, "Hello," Frank wouldn't reply. Other times, Harry would be preparing dinner and Frank would step into the kitchen and stand, his arms crossed and when Harry would glance back at him, Frank would let out a frustrated snort, turn and stomp back down the hallway.

When Harry returned home, he found Angie sitting on the stairs, her eyes red, tears on her cheeks. As he opened the door to the foyer, she leapt up and started up the stairs, but when she saw Harry, she sank back to a sitting position.

"What's wrong?" Harry said. He went to her and touched her shoulder then sat beside her, taking her hands.

"I'm okay," she said, struggling to maintain her composure. "No problem."

"Come on, you can tell me. It's Bill, right? What's he done?"

"It's not what he's done," she said. "It's what he doesn't do. I found out today that the job he keeps claiming he was up for was a lie. When I suggested he might want to find something else, he blew up — tore up the apartment and flew out of here." She put her head briefly on Harry's shoulder then lifted it again and finished, "Probably out getting tanked now."

"Stop worrying about him," Harry said. "He's not worth it."

"But what if he doesn't come back?"

"I'd say you'd be a lot better off," Harry said and smiled. He stood and said, "Come on, I'll make us some coffee — we can talk."

"I don't know," she said, looking away from him.

"Come on," he said, gently tugging her arm. She finally stood and he led her to the door. He unlocked it, admitted her and was in the process of closing it when he remembered Frank. Harry kicked the door shut and rushed after Angie but reached her a moment too late. She gasped loudly, but before the scream could leave her throat, Harry clamped his hand over her mouth and pulled her back down the hallway. She fell against him, hysterical.

"Harry — my god — we've — my god — the police!"

"No," Harry said. "No police." He gripped her arms tightly as she struggled.

"No — police?" she said, staring at him with a look of horrified puzzlement. "My god Frank's — Harry, we've got to —"

"No," he said. "I did it."

Angie fell silent, staring into his eyes. Slowly, her head started to shake, and she jerked away from him and fell against the wall.

"No — no, no, no," she said, shaking her head violently.

"Yes. I had to. I had no choice."

"You killed him?" Not facing him, she said, "Why?"

"For god's sake, you know what he was like," Harry burst out. "Try living with that all the time."

"But you killed him?"

"It wasn't that hard," he said calmly. "No, that was the easy part."

She turned toward the kitchen.

"No, Angie, don't," Harry said, grabbing for her arm.

"I want to see him," she said coolly.

Harry waited a moment then followed her. She was standing a few feet from Frank's body, her hand over her mouth, her eyes pinned on the gash in his head.

"It's pretty ugly," she said, with difficulty. She turned to Harry, "But not as bad as you might think."

She moved slowly toward Harry and said, "How did it feel?"

"What?"

"When you did it, how'd it feel?"

He shrugged.

"I don't know. It didn't feel like anything, really. It went pretty fast."

She pointed at the frying pan on the table, saying, "That's what you used?" Not waiting for a response, "Just like in the movies."

"Yeah, I guess."

"This is all so freaky," she said. "But exciting, you know?" She walked to Harry and put her hand on his chest. "And you just did it like that?"

"Yeah," he said, "best way, really." He looked into her eyes and said, "It works best for a lot of things."

They were staring deeply into each other's eyes. Angie leaned toward Harry and they fell into a passionate kiss.

Angie pitched her head back and gasped then let out a long sigh and fell to the bed beside Harry, laying her head on his shoulder and rubbing his chest. He turned and kissed her on the forehead then they lay silently for a few minutes.

"God, I haven't felt like that in a long time," she said, "a damn long time."

"Bill not much in that department?"

"Bill's not much in any department."

"I don't get the fascination," Harry said. "What's he got?"

"Hard to say anymore," she said, moving her hand to his chest. "At first, when I met him, he was great. Good sense of humor — had a really good job in construction. Then after he lost it —"

"He lost it," Harry concluded.

"You bet he did," she said. "Started drinking, staying out late. I keep thinking he'll change. Go back to the way he was."

"I think it's time you made a change," Harry said.

Angie raised her head then lowered it close to Harry's, saying, "I might." She kissed him then laughed, finally laying her head on his chest.

Harry sat on his couch again, staring at the lifeless legs of his now ex-roommate. Angie had left a short while before, when they heard Bill come in and stumble upstairs. Harry sensed the tension in Angie when they first heard the front door open and as soon as the upstairs door shut, she sprang from the bed and proceeded to dress quickly.

"What's going on?" Harry said. "You're not —"

"I have to," she said, "at least for now."

She paused then leaned back down and kissed him.

"Plan still the same?" he said. "Midnight?"

"On the dot," Angie replied. "I'll make sure Bill can't walk by then."

With that she left, and Harry heard her leave the apartment. He also heard a short time later when she returned and the commotion her arrival upstairs caused. Bill wasn't happy about her not being there when he came in, but apparently whatever she had bought at the store appeased him for he only raged for fifteen minutes before quieting down.

No longer concerned for her immediate safety, Harry had time to consider the plan they had worked out for disposing of Frank. Angie would work to make sure Bill was incoherent by midnight then the two of them would get Frank's body into the basement where they'd find some way to bury him. The landlord had recently had men working on the sewage system and they'd left behind an assortment of picks and shovels as well as several large holes in the concrete which Angie felt would provide a nice final resting place for Frank.

Harry stood and went into the kitchen and made a cup of instant coffee then sat at the table. He leaned his head on his hands and stared hard at the inanimate body of Frank. He tried but could not summon up what the final straw had been, what last indignity on Frank's part had forced Harry to raise that frying pan above his head and strike that final blow. Perhaps there had not been one thing, no final straw but a continuous stream of shocks to the system which had worn Harry down over time. He had always considered himself a patient man, but he knew his patience had its limits and he came to realize early on that Frank was just the person to test those limits.

Frank was the sort who could leave nothing as he found it — he was always tinkering, changing things but never for any good reason. A week after he moved in, Frank rearranged the kitchen without consulting Harry, putting the silverware in different drawers and moving the table out of the breakfast nook where it had always been to the middle of the kitchen where it made maneuvering the kitchen difficult. He changed things simply because he had not designed them and could not live comfortably with them as they were.

Frank wasn't much better at conversation. He was like a child, always saying "Why?" to every statement and arguing just to hear himself talk. He'd take any statement Harry made and pounce on it, picking it apart, trying to force Harry into making a misstatement as though their conversations were debates where Frank could gain the upper hand. Harry had stopped having lengthy conversations with Frank, restricting discussions to little more than simple questions and answers, usually about household duties.

When it came to those duties, Frank was better at criticizing the way Harry handled his share than he was at handling his own share of the work. Both cleaned the bathroom at intervals, but it was Frank who sat down one night and drew up a set of guidelines to follow while cleaning it — guidelines which Frank usually failed to follow, and he was always very good at spotting areas Harry missed, which usually prompted a nasty note which was posted on the bathroom mirror outlining areas where Harry was lacking. Harry felt the common areas, such as the bathroom and kitchen should be cleaned when necessary; Frank felt they should be cleaned on a regular schedule whether messy or not. He always insisted the trash be taken out on Tuesday, regardless of whether or not the bag was full.

Harry knew early on that things weren't working out and decided that one of them had to go.

"Fine, if that's how you feel," Frank said when Harry brought it up. "But I'll expect you to help me find another roommate."

"What?" Harry said. "You think I'm going to move?"

"You're the one with the problem," Frank replied. "I don't think it's fair to make me move when you're the one who can't get along."

"But I was here first!" Harry exclaimed.

"I'm not moving," Frank said angrily. "So, I suppose you'll just have to shape up."

It had been the last time they'd attempted to discuss the situation, in fact, the last time they'd discussed anything at all. The notes continued, but Harry largely ignored them as well as the majority of his duties around the house. Frank in turn began keeping track of every local call he made, saying he was "tired of covering" Harry and he started leaving notes about the electric bill, saying he didn't think it was "fair" for him to pay half when Harry was the one who kept his lights and stereo on late at night. All more shocks for Harry to absorb.

"I'm only surprised I didn't kill you sooner, lousy asshole," Harry said to his dead roommate. "You bastard, you should've gotten out while you had the chance."

Shortly after midnight, Angie descended into the basement and unlocked the rear door. She exited through it, tapping quickly on the rear door of Harry's apartment and re-entering the basement. Shortly after that, she heard something being dragged across the floor above, followed by a variety of curses then the sound of a door opening. Several minutes passed before Harry appeared in the doorway of the basement, stood up straight and wiped his brow.

"Bastard's heavier than you might think," he said.

"Hurry as much as you can," Angie said in a loud whisper.

"Yes, dear," Harry said sarcastically. "Have you picked out a spot?"

Angie looked around then went to a spot in the basement where there had obviously been some digging lately. She knelt and ran her hands through the dirt then stood up and said, "Dirt's pretty loose over here. This shouldn't take long."

Harry nodded and bent over again and resumed dragging Frank. In the time since he and Angie hatched their plan, Harry had wrapped the body in black plastic trash bags which he had sealed with duct tape. He had sprayed the whole body with Lysol before wrapping, though he doubted that would have done much for any smells. Fortunately, it had been rather cool, so Frank had remained well-preserved in the meantime. Once Harry had him in the basement, he grabbed some shovels and joined Angie at the spot she'd chosen.

"You think there are any pipes down there?" he said.

"Gosh, I don't know," she said. "Maybe."

"Well, there's only one way to find out," Harry said and started digging. Angie watched him a second then began digging as well. They worked for over an hour, carefully looking for and bypassing any pipes they found, until they had an oblong hole nearly six feet long and very deep. Harry straightened, holding his lower back.

"I think it's good enough," he said.

"Are you sure," Angie said, rubbing her left shoulder and moving around to stretch out her back. "I mean, we want to be sure he stays down here."

"It's good enough," Harry said. "Nobody's going to be digging around here after this. Besides, when they're finished, they're going to put cement back on top."

Angie considered this a minute or so then nodded.

"I don't look forward to refilling this hole," she said.

"Tell me about it," Harry agreed.

He crawled from the hole then extended his hand and helped her out. Then he went to Frank and started to drag the body over. Neither had heard the commotion upstairs, nor noted the footsteps above them or on the basement steps. Both were startled by Bill's voice, however.

"What the hell is going on down here?" Bill said, emerging from the shadows. "What you got there?"

Angie gasped and tried to intercept Bill. He roughly pushed her aside and went to where Harry stood.

"I'll be damned," Bill said, looking from the body to Harry and back. "This is my lucky day after all."

"What are you talking about?" Harry said.

"All day long, I've been thinking where I'm going to make some damn money, but now I ain't got to worry no more," he replied.

"You think I'm going to give you money?" Harry said.

"Damn right," Bill said. "Or else the cops are going to love hearing what I have to tell them."

Harry rushed Bill, knocking him back, but not off his feet. They fought for several minutes, before Bill managed a strong glancing right to Harry's jaw which sent him sprawling to the floor.

"Son of a bitch!" Bill said, grabbing a shovel and raising it over his head as he advanced on Harry. "You son of a —"

He did not finish. Instead, his shoulders hunched, and a look of pain crossed his face and he let out a short, "Arrgh!" Bill released the shovel then stood, motionless, for half a moment then dropped, first to his knees, then face down, a pickaxe squarely embedded in his back. Angie, trembling violently, stood just behind him.

Harry jumped up and rushed to Angie, taking her in his arms.

"I couldn't —" she said blankly. "I couldn't let him hurt you."

"It's okay," Harry said pressing his head against hers. "Everything's going to be okay."

As Harry left for work, he heard Angie in the foyer, talking to someone whose voice Harry recognized. He opened his apartment door and saw Angie with a Pakistani fellow Harry recognized as Mr. Singh, the landlord.

"I can't possibly afford it," Angie was saying.

"What's up?" Harry said brightly.

"Miss Stevenson informs me that her roommate has gone, and we were discussing the disposition of the upstairs apartment," said Mr. Singh.

"Bill's gone?" Harry said.

Angie, somewhat flustered, replied, "He left a week or so ago, but I thought he'd be back. Last night, he left a message on the machine saying he was in Mexico and wouldn't be calling again."

"You're kidding," Harry said. "Hang on a minute, will you?"

He went back into his apartment and reemerged with a note composed on a computer.

"I found this on the bathroom mirror the other day," he said as he handed it to Mr. Singh.

"Harry," Singh read aloud. "I've decided to return to Massachusetts. My plane departs this a.m. I know this is short notice, but I can't help that. You may keep whatever of my furnishings you want, but I expect compensation. Frank."

"I guess when it rains, it pours, huh?" Harry said.

"Well you still have six months left on your lease," Singh told him. "You can't break it."

Harry shrugged. "I guess I'll start looking."

"Wait," Singh said, suddenly deep in thought. Angie gave Harry a questioning look.

"Would the two of you consider doubling up?" Singh said.

Almost at the same time, Angie and Harry said, "What?"

"I don't know about that," Angie said.

"Yeah," Harry echoed. "It would be kind of weird."

"Not at all," said Singh. "I would honor the terms of your current lease and it would give me the opportunity to rent the top apartment at a higher rate."

Angie shook her head then looked at Harry and said, "I don't take up too much space. I'm sure we could work something out."

Harry thought about it then said, "Okay, let's say I won't rule it out."

"Excellent!" said Singh, clapping his hands. "I'm sure we can come to a satisfying conclusion for all concerned."

Metempsychosis

The phone was ringing when Katy entered her apartment. She let two rings pass as she set her bags of groceries onto the table and placed her jacket on the back of a chair. She answered amid the third ring to be greeted by a dial tone. After replacing the receiver, she stood over the phone a moment, trying to remember if she'd asked anyone to call her. She decided she had not and set about unpacking her groceries.

She set the cans of tuna, potted meat, SpaghettiOs and various soups she'd purchased into a crate on the floor of the kitchenette which sat beside another crate filled with pots, pans, plates and silverware. She carefully folded the empty bags and placed them between the crates. The phone rang and Katy turned toward it, waiting for another ring which didn't come. She stepped into the bathroom and unbuttoned her blouse then turned on the hot water and waited until steam was rising from the sink before putting her hands under. She winced at first but held her hands under the flow until she could not feel the heat and rubbed her hands. Then she turned off the water and shook her hands dry.

Katy looked at herself in the mirror. She had a small head, but a large face, with thin, dark eyebrows and a long nose, bent slightly in the middle from where she broke it at age five going down a slide the wrong way. Her lips were full and, when opened, revealed large, perfectly straight white teeth. Her eyes didn't match, one was hazel, the other a pale blue, and as a child, she sometimes scared the other children in the neighborhood by telling them that her different color eyes meant she was a witch.

She leaned close to the mirror and touched the small, nearly unnoticeable scar above her top lip, to the right. She tried recalling where it came from, but couldn't, beyond deciding it was either the result of a bike crash at age ten, where she bit through her lip, or from falling against a barbed wire fence at age thirteen. Her little sister had tripped her, and Katy missed hitting her eye by less than an inch. She covered her left eye and looked around the room, trying to imagine what things would look like if she had lost it.

She stood straight and viewed herself in the mirror again, this time running her hands behind her neck, and grasping the ends of her hair, which just barely touched the base of her head. She moved her fingers through her hair, starting from back to front, trying to puff it up and finally shaking her head.

"Got to grow the hair back," she said and left the bathroom.

Katy sat on the bed, a rollaway that she almost never rolled away. She untied, and carefully removed her shoes, placing them, side by side, just under the bed so that only the points of the toes stuck out. She unsnapped her jeans, black like her blouse, but did not unzip them, nor did she remove her blouse. There was a creak from above and she looked quickly up, listening for an indication that the upstairs neighbor was home. No sounds followed, and she sighed, laid back onto the bed, allowing one leg to drape over the side. She ran the tips of her fingers along her waist, under the top of her jeans then dangled her arm over the side of the bed, folding her other arm under the back of her neck.

Katy had been born in Fort Lauderdale, Florida, but never quite felt at home in the "Sunshine State." With dark hair and cream-colored skin — she burned easily — she hardly evoked the healthy, tanned image commonly associated with palm trees and citrus fruits. She hated orange juice, couldn't swim and had long preferred sitting in a library reading Poe or Plath to lying on a beach developing skin cancer. She enjoyed dressing in layers, and hardly ever went out without wearing a jacket or overcoat, sometimes an overcoat over a jacket.

Katy preferred an uncluttered existence and surrounded herself with few things. Her furnishings included the bed, a dresser with an attached mirror, and a fold-up card table that Katy found on Mott Street. She had two mismatched chairs around the table.

The studio had a bathroom and an attached kitchenette with a sink, stove and a few cabinets which Katy rarely used, rarely even opened. She liked to have everything out where she could see it. Katy read a lot but did not own any books. Instead she took weekly, sometimes daily trips to the public library when she wanted to read.

From above came the sound of a door slamming, followed by the heavy clump of feet hitting the floor. The sound stopped near the center of the ceiling and a moment later, two thumps came. Then the footsteps started again, but this time it was the thud of bare feet on the wooden floor.

Katy sighed and said softly but firmly, "Dominguez."

She had never met the upstairs neighbor, nor was she entirely sure if it was a man or woman who lived above her. One afternoon, however, while collecting her mail, Katy glanced at the mailbox for the upstairs apartment and saw a yellowed slip of paper, the name "Dominguez" written on it, taped above the mailbox. From then on, she began to refer to the person upstairs by that name. The apartment had formerly been occupied by Dominguez, a relatively quiet person with a cat that meowed all day. But that Dominguez had moved and had been replaced by a new Dominguez. This one was much larger, judging by how forcefully his feet hit the floor, and kept irregular hours, and, as soon as this Dominguez came in each evening, he always cranked up the stereo. As if on cue, Katy's room was filled with Caribbean music.

Katy put her hand over her face and rolled onto her stomach, pulling her arms to either side of her head. She had never liked the music that came from above, never liked the sounds of Dominguez's feet hitting the floor as he danced about to the music, but there wasn't much Katy could do. A week after the new Dominguez moved in, Katy went up to complain about the music, but as soon as she tapped on the door, the music stopped, but no one came to the door.

She called out, "Hello? Hey, I know you're there," but was ignored.

After she'd gone back downstairs, Dominguez waited a full five minutes before turning the music back on and it had gone on this way ever since.

Katy had come to New York two years earlier, hoping on the one hand to escape the dismal cheerfulness of South Florida and on the other hand to lose herself among the hustle of 8 million people. Stepping off the Greyhound at Port Authority, she immediately felt small and insignificant among the buildings and this feeling appealed to her. She felt that if she wanted to scream at the top of her lungs, she could do so at any point during the day at any place in the city and no one would notice. Emotional outbursts were not her style, however. Katy was at her happiest on days when she didn't have to leave the apartment or exchange words with anyone.

When Katy boarded the bus in Florida, she had long hair and was wearing a yellow sundress. Back then, she had been Katherine Hagan — but only for about ten years. Katy's parents divorced when she was six and her mother married Arthur Hagan a few months before Katy turned eight. Arthur had never formally adopted Katy or her sister, but the two were enrolled in school under his name and that was how all Katy's classmates had known her. Her mother and Arthur put Katy on the bus, bound for North Carolina, thinking she was off to visit an aunt Katy hadn't seen since childhood.

When she set out, Katherine Hagan had intended to go to North Carolina then work her way up the coast to New York. But while she was on a stopover in Atlanta, Katy looked at herself in the mirror and had not seen Katherine Hagan anymore, but Katy McCoy, and that's who she became. After that, nothing was right — she felt changed, as though she was someone new. Now she had to look the part.

She bought a pair of scissors from the gift shop and cut off as much of her hair as she could then recovered her bags from the bus and changed clothes, finally giving the sundress to an old woman begging change in the terminal.

She returned to the ladies' room and looked in the mirror a final time and said, "Where does Katy McCoy want to go?"

Katy traded in her ticket for one to New York. She hadn't spoken to her mother since, though Katy sent a postcard a few weeks after arriving in New York. It was a blank card on which she wrote, "Don't worry. I'm fine."

She spent her first several days in New York in a half-star hotel on Times Square, living out of her single suitcase until the desk attendant stopped her one afternoon and mentioned that the credit card she'd used when registering had been reported stolen. She'd "borrowed" it from Donny, her last boyfriend, the day before she left for New York. Katy explained to the desk attendant that there had been a "big mistake" and she would correct the situation immediately. That afternoon, she dropped her suitcase out of the third story window then snuck down the back steps. For the next two months, she slept at the Y, and looked for a job.

Katy eventually found a position at a record store, where her main duties included explaining the nuances of new age music to people so accustomed to hard rock that Katy often had to raise her voice to be heard. One afternoon, she overheard Steve, one of the guys who delivered records to the store, telling someone about how much money he made illegally subletting his apartment. Steve mentioned where the place was, and Katy made an "anonymous" call to the manager of the building. By the end of the week, Steve and his sublet were kicked out. The day after that, Katy showed up looking for a room. She had been in the apartment ever since.

Katy rose and went to the kitchenette. She bent over and surveyed the cans she had placed there a short while earlier but could not decide on anything to eat. She went to the refrigerator and removed a loaf of white bread then took out four slices, folded them over and mashed them into a cylindrical shape then took a bite out of one end. Chewing, she returned to the bed and sat.

The music from Dominguez's apartment had stopped about ten minutes after Katy heard Dominguez in the shower. Just after the music stopped, the door slammed again and Katy heard Dominguez running down the steps near her apartment, but she had not attempted to see Dominguez. For a week after she had gone up to complain about the music, Katy had entertained the notion that she'd like to know who lived upstairs. The curiosity she felt was much stronger than for the previous Dominguez, who Katy had hardly noticed at all. The new one was different. He had invaded Katy's private space with his music, and she felt justified in seeing who it was. To this end, she would rush out with a half-full bag of trash or down to check her mailbox whenever she heard Dominguez' door slam.

Katy developed a new plan shortly afterward, however, and she stopped trying to see Dominguez. In fact, she went to the opposite extreme and made every effort not to see him. Katy decided that since Dominguez had violated her space with the music then she would strike back by making Dominguez whatever she wanted him to be. She used what little she knew of Dominguez to start with — the feet on the floor. They struck the wood heavily, more than a simple, natural stride would cause and one step followed another quickly. Katy decided Dominguez was large, somewhat paunchy, and the music made him Jamaican, though Katy opted for short hair, which she preferred, to long dreadlocks. Dominguez would be black, with black eyes and blue-black hair. Katy could never decide on a job, however. Sometimes she felt construction, other times she went with artist, perhaps the guy who she saw in the West Village who did caricatures of people.

Katy was still dressed, and she rose again and went to the closet and took out a red terrycloth housecoat. This was one of the few articles of clothing she'd brought from Florida that she still had. She usually preferred wearing only the housecoat when she was home, forsaking even shoes. The robe had a rip in it that started between the shoulders and went down to the small of her back and she had made attempts to sew it, only to have it rip beside the stitches she'd put in. She hadn't washed the robe since coming to New York.

She took off her blouse and hung it in the closet then slowly unzipped her jeans and slid them down and stepped out of them. She folded them carefully, smoothing them with her hands on the table. Then she put her jeans on a hanger in the closet. There was a full-sized mirror on the closet door and Katy stood in front of it as she removed her bra and panties. Then she dropped her arms to her side and examined herself, first from the front then the side.

She was less than five feet tall without shoes, but alone she rarely noticed her height. When she was out, she had learned to deal with her diminutive size by walking as forcefully as she could. No crowd was too thick for Katy to muscle her way through. There were four or five homeless men who begged just outside the doorway of Katy's store and they could be very obnoxious, jumping into people's faces as they left with their purchases. When the beggars saw Katy, her head down, hands thrust into her coat pockets, they stepped aside.

She ran her hand up and down her stomach then traced her ribs and ran her hands down her sides to her hips.

"Still not eating enough," she said. She shrugged and put on the robe.

Katy looked at herself in the mirror again and touched her hair, first softly stroking it then running her fingers into it until they ran, roughly, along her scalp. She pulled her hair straight back, holding it with both hands and narrowed her eyes then pouted. She went into the bathroom and wet her hair then combed it back and returned to the mirror. First, she stood sideways, shoving her hands into the pockets of the robe and turning her face to the mirror. She retrieved her sunglasses from the dresser and put them on, resuming the pose. She laughed then took off the glasses and replaced them on the dresser.

She paused at the dresser and leaned her head on one arm, picking up items with her free hand. There were two unopened ten packs of tokens and she examined them to be sure there were ten in each pack. Then she picked up a soiled Polaroid snapshot of a nude woman standing by a refrigerator. Katy didn't know the woman but had found the photo on the B-train one afternoon — someone put it in one of the empty ad frames. She looked at another of a man and woman, their faces pressed together filling the entire picture. Katy didn't know them either. She collected pictures of people she didn't know. Usually she'd swipe them from work, party pictures of former employees, snapshots of people's children. Sometimes she'd get a thrill just out of stealing the picture: planning the snatch, making sure no one was watching, and then stuffing it into her pockets. Mostly, though, she just grabbed them quickly, whenever she'd see one she liked. She kept the most interesting ones on top of the dresser, where she could see them all the time; the others she stashed in a shoe box.

Her thoughts were interrupted by the phone. She looked at it as it rang twice then a third time. Before the fourth ring, she picked up and, in a voice lower than normal, said, "Yeah?"

"Katherine Hagan?" the man's voice said.

Katy hesitated then, in the same voice as before, said, "No, wrong number."

She sat on the bed and sighed. She did not recognize the voice on the phone and wondered who it was. She decided that there were hundreds of Katy McCoys in New York, so if someone was trying to track her down it would take forever. If someone really wanted to find her, she was sure she would have heard from someone before this. Katy closed her eyes and laid on the bed.

She heard a creak from above, followed by quickly moving feet, a sharp tap that sounded like high heels, followed by the thud of Dominguez' feet.

"Entertaining, are we?" Katy said.

The music started, but it was softer and slower than usual. This was accompanied by the high heel tap again and Dominguez' feet sliding nearby.

Katy stood and removed her robe then laid on her back on the bed. She rested her hands on her stomach then moved them upward, gliding them over her breasts. She closed her eyes but did not think of anything or anybody, just the sensation of her own hands on her body.

She moved one hand down to her stomach then between her legs, rubbing faster and faster until the orgasm hit, and she arched her back and gasped. Then she relaxed and rolled to her side, curling into a ball. She fell into a deep sleep while above, the music continued, accompanied by the thump of bare feet on the wooden floor.

Route 412 to Tulsa

"No!" Mary shrieked as the car began to sputter. "Not again."

The car barely had enough power to get her to the side of the road where she stopped. This was the third time in as many days that the car had failed her. This time it was pitch-black outside.

Mary slammed her hands against the steering wheel, saying, "Stupid car — stupid."

The previous day she visited a used car lot and nearly traded in her old Chevy for a newer model. After considering the expense, she decided that her car had somehow gotten her from Atlanta to Los Angeles. She was sure it could get her back.

Mary looked at her watch. It was nearly ten-o-clock and she had no idea where she was though she knew she was in Oklahoma. The last sign she saw indicated she was headed toward Tulsa where she had hoped to rest for the evening. Now she regretted her decision to take the back roads instead of the Interstate.

See the country — yeah, right.

She couldn't remember the last time she'd seen a car on this road.

Mary sat back and stared into the darkness, broken only by her headlights. She'd left Atlanta two months ago to drive across country to visit her parents. They offered to pay for a plane ticket, but Mary wanted an adventure, something she could tell her kids someday. She was disappointed that she'd seen little of the surrounding area via Interstate and decided to take the "scenic route" on the return trip. She hadn't listened to her parents, who cautioned her about driving alone in unknown territories.

The first time the car broke down it had been something simple, something to do with the distributor, the mechanic had said. He offered to check the car for other problems, but Mary had been in a hurry and had declined. The next time it was the alternator and the mechanic replaced it. Now as she sat there recalling the repairs, she resolved that when she got to Tulsa, she'd visit the first used car lot she could find and get something more reliable.

Mary checked her watch again then debated whether or not she should try to walk to get help or stay where she was. She didn't know how close the nearest town was and wasn't sure anything would be open and thought that it would be safer to stay in the car. She sat back and grabbed a strand of her long brown hair and began twirling it in her fingers.

She must have dozed off because the next thing she was aware of was the sound of someone tapping on her window. She opened her eyes to see an old man with a flash-light peering in. Mary rolled down the window.

"Looks like you've had some car trouble," the old man said. "Anything I can do to help?"

"You wouldn't happen to have a tow truck, would you?" Mary asked. She looked ahead to the dark sedan parked in front of her.

No, of course not.

"I could give you a lift into the next town," the man told her. "The garage won't be open but maybe you could find a place to sleep."

Mary looked the old man over. He was around six feet tall with thinning gray hair and wearing wire-framed glasses. He was wearing a plaid shirt and light-colored slacks. Mary was reminded of her grandfather.

How dangerous can he be?

"Sure, I'd like that."

She rolled up the window and opened the door. The man stood back, shining his light on her until she was out. She locked the door and followed the man to his car. The inside was warm, and the seat was soft leather and the whole interior had a light pine smell. Again, Mary thought about her grandfather. This was just the sort of car he'd have.

The old man got in and put the car in drive.

"Where exactly am I?" Mary said.

"This is route four twelve," the man said, "takes you right into Tulsa." He glanced over at her and continued, "So what's a young woman like yourself doing out on a deserted road at this time of night?"

"I'm on my way to Atlanta. I attend school there."

The man nodded. "I'm Bernard Johnson, by the way."

"Mary Reeves."

"I sort of figured that you're not from around here," he said.

"No, I'm from Santa Monica. I was visiting my parents."

"What brought you out here?" he asked.

"I wanted to see the country." There was a slight hint of sarcasm in her voice.

"Bet your parents are worried about you," he said.

"Not really. They think I'm taking the expressway. I should have."

"It's not safe for a young woman out here on her own," Mr. Johnson said. "No telling what could happen."

The comment made Mary slightly uncomfortable.

I'm being paranoid. There's nothing to worry about.

"Do you live around here?"

"Not far." He was concentrating on the road and not looking at Mary when he spoke.

"I'm sure it's beautiful country in the daytime."

He nodded staring straight ahead.

In the distance, Mary could see the sign for a motel. She felt relieved.

"Oh, good, there's a place."

Mr. Johnson continued to stare straight ahead.

Surely, he sees the motel.

When they got to the driveway, he didn't slow down.

"Hey, you missed the turn."

"There'll be other places," he told her.

Mary's mind started racing.

What have I gotten myself into?

Where is this guy taking me?

What will happen when we get there?

Mary looked into the side mirror at the motel vanishing in the distance, and then noticed they were going very fast. "You should watch out. The cops might pull you over."

"Don't see many police out this way," he said calmly, "especially at this time of night."

Mary felt her heart pounding. Her hands were shaking.

How can I get away?

Should I wait until we get wherever we're going and try to run, or should I try to jump out?

The fall might kill me.

Hell, this guy will most likely kill me when we get where we're going.

I can't just wait for something to happen.

I'll have to make something happen.

Mary ran several scenarios through her mind until she came up with one that might work. She slowly reached down and unhooked her seatbelt. Mr. Johnson continued staring at the road and didn't seem to notice what she was doing. The road they were on was bordered by trees and high grass.

Suddenly, Mary reached over and grabbed the steering wheel, jerking it roughly to the right.

"What the—" Mr. Johnson said as he tried to steady the car. It skidded across the road a time or two before running off the road into a ditch.

Mary opened the door and sprang from the car, running toward the tree line. She lost her footing and fell into the tall grass and started crawling. Behind her she could hear the car door open and close again. She stopped moving and turned so she could see the car.

Mr. Johnson was walking toward her with his flashlight. He scanned the area and the light ran right in front of where Mary was hiding.

"A young woman shouldn't be out here all alone," Mr. Johnson said loudly, his voice calm. "It's not safe."

He started walking again and Mary could hear him coming closer. She held her breath and tried to remain perfectly still as he stopped just a few feet from where she was laying and she could hear him whistling an indistinct tune as he searched for her.

Johnson remained standing just a few feet from her until Mary thought her lungs would burst then he started walking again. She could hear his footsteps moving farther and farther away and she slowly let out her breath. Finally, she heard gravel crunching under his feet as he headed back to the car still whistling. She heard one door close then the other and she let out a relieved sigh when she heard the car pull out onto the highway.

Mary stayed where she was until the sun came up. She rose to her knees and looked around and, seeing no one, stood. She took a few moments to look herself over. Her hands and the front of her jeans were dirty, and she wiped them off before walking back toward the motel. All the time she kept looking over her shoulder for a dark sedan.

At the motel, she found a man at the front desk. "My car broke down and I need to call a tow truck."

He gave her a long stare and replied, "How did you get here?"

"I walked."

"It's not safe walking around out there by yourself," the desk attendant said. "The slasher might have gotten you."

"The slasher?"

"Yes, the 412 Slasher," the desk attendant said. "At least that's what the TV news calls him."

He explained to Mary that over the past twenty years there had been dozens of women murdered along that stretch of Highway 412. All had their throats cut. The desk attendant broke off his story and said, "Are you all right? You just turned white as a sheet."

Mary's heart was pounding; she was trembling. She felt a gnawing sensation in the pit of her stomach. "Forget the tow truck. I think I need to talk to the police."

The Keys to Success

For the first time in his life, Scott Brown doesn't know where his keys are. Actually, he does know where they are; they're in his car but he doesn't know where his car is. He'd left the bar in Buckhead where he and his friends had been hanging out and had just unlocked the door to his car when a guy who couldn't have been more than sixteen or seventeen years old stuck a gun in his face and said, "Give me your keys!"

Scott complied.

Now he is waiting for the police to arrive so he can make a statement and be told that they'll do all they can to find his vehicle, though Scott is certain he'll never again see his car in one piece. At least he doesn't have to wait alone. Becky, a woman he was talking to in the bar came along a few minutes after the car-jacking and has remained with Scott to console him.

"You poor thing," Becky says. "You must have been so scared."

"I didn't have time to be scared," Scott says. "It happened so fast."

"Well you're handling it well," Becky says. "I'd be a mess right now."

"You'd do fine, I'm sure," Scott says.

Running into Becky has been the highlight of an otherwise unpromising evening for Scott. He'd spoken to her in the bar, but she never gave the impression she was that interested in him. Plus, she mentioned a "situation" with her boyfriend who sometimes wanted to see other people. Scott decided he'd done okay as he had spoken to her for nearly twenty minutes before she mentioned her boyfriend, so he had considered that a minor success until she showed up in the parking lot and approached him a few minutes after his car had been taken.

Becky Shaughnessy lives up to her Irish name with auburn hair and green eyes. She's dressed for a night on the town, wearing a short dark skirt and a blue halter-style top with two-inch red pumps which accentuate her already tall stature. Scott's reasonably tall himself with blonde hair and brown eyes. He was happy to meet someone he didn't have to look down at and in fact it was her height which first attracted him to her.

They'd talked about trivial things, where they went to school, where they'd been raised, what they did for a living. It was here where Becky invoked the boyfriend when Scott told her he was an accountant.

"Craig works for H&R Block," she said. "He's really busy this time of year."

"Yes, we're all busy in March and April," Scott said. "So, you have a boyfriend."

"Kind of," Becky replied. "We're sort of on-again, off-again."

"Where are you now?" Scott asked.

"Hard to say," she replied.

They'd spoken for a few more minutes before Scott excused himself to catch up with his friends. He left the bar ten minutes later and had his fateful run-in with the carjacker. Becky arrived about five minutes later. Scott is happy for the company even though he's pretty sure he won't get much further with Becky. Since arriving, though, she's seemed much more interested in him than she was in the bar.

The police arrive and Scott gives them a description of his car and the carjacker as well as his license number. Becky stands to the side, patiently waiting as Scott gives his statement. The police put out an APB on his car and tell him they'll do all they can to recover it then they ask him if he has a way to get home.

Before Scott can say anything, Becky steps over and says, "I can take him home."

Once the police have gone, Becky says, "Come on, my car's over here."

Scott follows her, saying, "You sure you don't mind taking me?"

"Not at all," Becky says, stopping and rubbing his arm. "It might give us a chance to get to know one another a little better."

"What about your on-again off-again situation?" Scott asks.

Smiling, Becky says, "It's always been more off than on. So where do you live?"

Twenty minutes later, they're entering Scott's condo in Brookhaven.

"This is a nice place!" Becky says as she looks around.

"It should be," Scott says. "It costs enough."

"I know what you mean," she says. "I refinanced a year ago and my payments are still through the roof."

"Would you like something to drink?" he says.

"Coke, Pepsi, whatever you have," she replies.

He gets them set up with drinks then they retire to the couch where they resume their conversation.

"You said you're from Atlanta," Becky says. "I haven't met many natives since I've been here."

"We're out there but you have to look carefully for us," Scott says with a chuckle. "Of course, a lot of people who say they're from Atlanta are actually from the suburbs, like Cobb or Gwinnett."

"That's where a lot of my co-workers are from," Becky says. "Some of them have commutes of an hour or more."

"I don't get that," Scott says. "I can understand wanting to live away from town, but you end up spending so much time on the road it almost doesn't seem worth it."

"Well I was lucky to find a place five minutes from where I work," she says. "I can practically walk."

"Sounds nice," he says. "So, tell me about this boyfriend who you may or may not be with."

Becky laughs. "It's not as complicated as it sounds. Craig and I have been dating for about two years, but he's never wanted to take it to the next level. I'm starting to get tired of waiting."

"Maybe he's just afraid of commitment," Scott says. "Some guys are like that."

"I don't think it's that," she says. "He's said he wants to get married someday. I just don't think he wants to marry me."

"That would be his loss, then," Scott says to which Becky smiles.

"What about you?" she says. "Are you seeing anyone?"

"You met me in a bar in Buckhead and you ask if I'm seeing anyone?" he says with a laugh.

"That doesn't always mean you're single," she answers, laughing as well. "Were you seeing anyone recently?"

"My last girlfriend was about six months ago," he says. "We got along okay, but she was never that committed to the relationship."

"Well it's her loss," Becky says. She props her arm onto the back of the couch and leans her head on her hand facing Scott. He turns so he's facing her.

He takes a sip of his drink. "You're from Massachusetts. What brought you down South?"

"I originally wanted to go to school," she says. "Georgia State has a good business program and I thought I'd get my MBA."

"Changed your mind?" he asks.

"I decided I didn't want to go to school any longer," she says. "After that I just decided to stay because I like it here."

"It can be a fun city if you know where to look," he says.

"You probably know lots of fun places," she says. "What do

you do for fun?"

"Go to movies, catch a play at the Shakespeare Tavern, watch the Braves," he says.

"I love Shakespeare," she says. "Maybe I can tag along sometimes."

"They're doing Hamlet next month," he says.

"It's a date then," she says.

They talk for nearly half an hour until their conversation is interrupted by the phone ringing.

"Hello?" Scott says when he picks up the phone. "Yes, this is he. Yes, it was taken earlier tonight. You did? That's great! So when can I pick it up?"

He finishes the call and says excitedly to Becky, "They found my car!"

"Yay!" she says, raising her arms in victory. "Where did they find it?"

"In a neighborhood about ten miles from where it was taken," he says.

Becky stands and goes to him and gives him a hug. "That's great. I'm sure you're relieved."

"I am," he says. "Listen, thanks for being there when I needed someone."

"No problem," she says. "I'm sure you would have done the same."

"I would have," he says. "At least it wasn't all bad."

"Yes," she says. She looks at her watch and says, "Oh, I should go. It's getting late."

They exchange telephone numbers and Scott walks her to the door.

"Thanks again for everything," he says. He opens the door for her. She lingers just inside the door for a few seconds.

"Now, you call me so we can see that play next month," she says.

"I hope I don't have to wait a month to see you again," he says.

"Call me," she says with a smile. "We'll see what comes up."

They are standing in the doorway looking at one another. Becky leans in and kisses him on the cheek then says, "See you."

Scott closes the door and stands there for a few minutes contemplating the evening.

"Maybe I should have my car stolen more often," he says.

Double Fault

Glenn Harmon was a tennis fan who had developed an unhealthy obsession with Serena Williams and had even gone so far as to look up her email address on the Internet. Unfortunately, the Serena Williams whose address he found was not the world-class tennis player, but a college sophomore at FSU, from Columbus, Georgia. To make matters worse, she was away on vacation when he began his one-sided correspondence, so that by the time she returned, her box was filled with lengthy missives, counseling her on how to improve her backhand, or consoling her over a loss. This Serena Williams was not a tennis fan and did not immediately make the connection. She wondered how she had garnered the attention of this possibly disturbed individual.

Wading through the megabytes of info, she found his notes to be incredibly detailed and frank. He wrote as though he actually knew the person he was addressing and had a long association with her. Serena decided if he did know the person he would, no doubt, have a correct email address for her.

It wasn't long after this curious episode began that Serena learned the truth, but rather than correct Glenn's misconception, she decided it would be fun to play along. She began crafting terse, boilerplate snippets thanking him for his support and apologizing for not being able to respond in detail. She never stopped to consider that she might be provoking a deranged stalker, liable to respond in any number of unpleasant ways. It was just a way for her to pass the time between classes.

Day after day, she labored to reply to his increasingly earnest entreaties and day after day her mailbox was filled with more of them. Having no idea about the "real life" of the person this man was trying to reach, Serena labored to come up with convincing answers to his rambling, yet detailed queries.

One such missive read, "What advice do you have for others trying to overcome obstacles to achieve their goals?"

"Hang in there and never get discouraged," Serena replied.

"I know you lived in Compton as a child, but I've had some trouble locating the block on which you lived," another email stated. "I've been scanning through old phone books from the time but there is more than one Richard Williams listed. Can you remember which house you lived in?"

More than a little disturbed by this line of inquiry, Serena replied, "I was pretty young then. I don't really remember the specific house."

In another, the poster sent an extremely long note asking for a comparison of one type of tennis ball to another.

"I generally use whatever the tour supplies," Serena replied.

"But what about practice?" the poster returned. "What do you prefer then?"

"Actually, the answer is the same," she said. "It's better to use what you're most likely to encounter during a tournament."

"Of course!" the poster sent back. "That makes perfect sense. Do you ever steal balls from the various tournaments?"

"Do you really believe I'd need to steal any?" she replied.

Another time he asked for detailed specs on the main court at Roland Garros. Not sure what he was talking about, Serena instead sent him a recipe for banana bread she had gotten from her grandmother.

"When I say I want a snack," she included in a note, "this is what you'd better be ready to bring me."

Was there any surprise that Serena arose one morning and found the news filled with stories of a demented individual trying to sneak into venues at the U.S. Open with 100 pounds of banana bread that he had baked himself? Did she feel at all responsible? Was this even the same man? She could not say.

Klan Candy

Being the public relations person for the Ku Klux Klan must be a thankless job at best. At worst, it's probably any PR person's living nightmare, somewhat akin to persuading the public that anthrax has many convenient household uses, or that, despite the unpleasantness, Hitler did encourage strong economic development. Charlie Watkins always marveled at these attempts to somehow add a positive spin to guys in sheets, waving Confederate flags around outside the local public assistance office, shouting "White power" at the top of their lungs.

He found himself pondering this as he held a bag of candy-coated chocolate drops — no doubt meant to be a generic knock-off of M&Ms — but emblazoned with three large, Gothic Ks and the tagline, "Join the Klan!"

The package ended up in his mailbox one Saturday morning, part of a varied assortment of sweets, all bearing the same message, and including an eight hundred number on the back of each packet to call for more information. Charlie wasn't sure how these folks had gotten into his subdivision. He'd never known any of his neighbors to belong to clandestine hate groups, but one could never be absolutely certain. Mr. Braxton over on Maple Lane did drive a pickup, and sometimes struck Charlie as a little too sympathetic to states' rights.

To learn more, Charlie visited the Paytons, his next-door neighbors, to see if they had received any candy. Marge Payton greeted him, and then retrieved a similar package of sweets that had arrived that same morning.

"What are we supposed to do with these?" she said. "It's not even good candy. What if the kids see this?"

"Why don't I just take it off your hands, Marge," Charlie offered.

"Really? You'd do that?"

"Sure, what are neighbors for?" Charlie said. "I'm guessing everyone on the block got one."

"Probably," Marge said. "Cynthia on the corner called me to say she got one."

Charlie turned to face the street. "Then I've got my work cut out for me."

He retrieved several Whole Foods bags from his garage, and then went to every house on his block, collecting candy. When he exhausted his block, he started hitting each street in the subdivision.

"Hello, I'm your neighbor, Charles Watkins," he'd say to whoever answered the door. "You wouldn't happen to have gotten a package of candy from the Klan today would you?"

After much success collecting candy in his subdivision, just for good measure, Charlie went into the next subdivision, where he was equally successful at finding the goods, accruing five bags full of it. He thought long and hard what to do with it, when an idea came to him.

Charlie got a couple of the large plastic jack-o-lanterns he put out for Halloween, filled them with the candy, placed the bags and jack-o-lanterns into his car, and headed off to the city.

Arriving at a gas station in town, Charlie spotted three large black men having an animated conversation at the air pump, while a fourth put air in the tire of a Chevy Suburban. Charlie parked nearby and approached them carrying one of the jack-o-lanterns.

"Could I interest you fellows in some Klan candy?" Charlie said.

The men looked around at one another and one said, "Klan candy? What the hell is that?"

"Candy distributed by the KKK," Charlie said, holding out the jack-o-lantern. "See? I found it in my subdivision this morning."

Each of the men took a packet and stared at it, and the one who'd spoken up, continued, "Why are you bringing this down here?"

"Just being neighborly," Charlie said. Pointing at one of the packets, he went on, "Oh, I failed to mention, there's a number on the back, where people can call and thank them for the candy."

The men looked on back and started to laugh. One of the other men, nodded emphatically.

"All right — we got you."

"There's plenty more where this came from," Charlie said. "Can I give you some to share with your friends."

One of the guys took a Publix bag from the Suburban.

"We'll do just that," the first man said.

After setting them up with lots of candy, Charlie drove around distributing the packets to anyone he could find hanging around at groceries, churches, gas stations, barbershops, and nail salons, then gave some to the mostly Spanish-speaking guys outside a home improvement store and left the remainder with the staff at the regional headquarters of the NAACP. Along the way, he made many new friends and amused countless individuals.

Once all the candy was gone, Charlie headed home, secure in the knowledge that he'd done his good deed for the day.

Back home, his wife Mira noted the missing bags. "So, you got rid of it all, eh?"

"I sure did," Charlie said. "I just hope the guys in the Klan appreciate all the work I did for them today."

"You're a humanitarian," Mira said, before letting Charlie know he wasn't off the hook for cutting the back yard that afternoon.

"A humanitarian's work is never done," he said with a sigh, before heading out back.

The Spitting Spiders of Borneo

In the pantheon of colorful characters, few could match Andy's uncle Calvin. A world traveler, Calvin would show up at family reunions every few years, full of stories of the odd cultures, and creatures he'd encountered in some distant land. This made him a perpetual favorite among the kids, and almost as soon as he stepped through the door, he'd herd the young folks together and immediately launch into a fascinating tale.

"Kids, have you ever heard of the spitting spiders of Borneo?" Calvin said with his characteristic bombast.

Heads shook.

Calvin leaned in and addressed them in a confidential tone. "Well, in Borneo, they have these giant spiders — and they spit!"

The adults never seemed to have much use for Calvin and were glad he spent the majority of his time regaling the children with his wild tales. Andy's father, Jack, in particular, dreaded Calvin's visits, claiming it wasn't out of the ordinary for Calvin to hit him up for money for some hare-brained scheme or another. Andy didn't care. He loved Uncle Calvin, and looked forward to Calvin's return.

"Andrew," Calvin would tell him, always using his full name, "a man needs adventure. Why, I hope I never grow too old to don the old fedora and take off for parts unknown."

Calvin was actually Andy's mother's uncle, the youngest of her father's siblings, born well after Andy's great-grandmother thought she could have more children, and was only a few years older than Andy's mother, Gloria. When Calvin wasn't around, Andy frequently heard his family say Calvin was spoiled as a child, his parents lacking the energy or motivation to discipline him. He grew up pampered, coddled, and with an unrealistic sense of his own importance.

Most of his brothers and sisters had left the house by the time he started school, so he had his parents' undivided attention, and so long as he didn't get into too much mischief, they were content to let him have his way. When he announced, shortly before he graduated high school, that he wanted to tour Africa, his parents were more than happy to send him off, so they could once again have the house to themselves.

From that point, it was one adventure after another for Calvin. No one in the family had any idea what Calvin did for a living. Inquiries about his employment status were often met with the cryptic, "I have many irons in the fire, let me tell you."

Whatever these were, Calvin kept them to himself. Jack generally tired of Calvin quickly, so his visits to the family were short.

One morning, while Calvin was staying with the family, Andy heard a knock at his door just as he was waking up.

"Come in," he called.

Calvin entered. Very dramatically, he tip-toed over to the bed, and crouched down so he'd be at eye-level with Andy.

"Up for a little adventure, Andrew?"

"What do you mean?" Andy asked, still sleepy.

"I'm off to track the elusive black mamba," Calvin said. "Thought you might like to tag along."

"Black mamba?" Andy said. "Is that a snake?"

"It certainly is," Calvin said. "It can outrun a cheetah! The terror of the forest."

"I don't think we should be fooling around with one of those," Andy said.

"Nonsense!" Calvin said. "I'm well-versed in how to handle myself around them. I could give you some pointers if we encounter one."

"Okay, I guess," Andy said. "Where do you want to go?"

"I thought we might take a hike around Mystic Lake," he said. "Perfect hunting grounds for our steely prey."

"Isn't that where they found the naked dead guy?" Andy asked.

"Indeed it is," Calvin replied. "Perhaps another victim of the elusive black mamba!"

"I don't think they're letting people go up there now."

"Son, nothing's off limits to men of adventure. Now get some hiking clothes on and let's hit the road."

When they arrived at the wilderness area, the road leading into it was closed, so Calvin parked just outside and retrieved a back-pack from the trunk.

"Andrew, my boy, looks like we're in for some hiking."

"I don't know if that's a good idea," Andy said. "They're pretty strict about people being up here."

"Not to worry," Calvin said, "you're with a responsible adult."

Not totally assured, Andy followed Calvin into the woods. They found a trail quickly and moved deeper into the forest. Along the way, Calvin would stop and point out some interesting type of foliage, or direct Andy's attention to a deer or other woodland creature. As they were circling back to find a place to rest and have some snacks, they were overtaken by a park ranger.

"Excuse me, what are you two doing out here? This part of the park is closed in the off season."

Calvin put his arm in front of Andy and said in a low voice, "Let me handle this, Andrew." Addressing the ranger, Calvin said, "You might say, we're on a botanical excursion."

"A botanical excursion," the man said. "What does that mean?"

Calvin sighed.

"If you must know, we're tracking the elusive black mamba."

"Black mamba — as in snake?"

"That is correct."

"What makes you think you'll find one out here?"

"Why, this is the perfect habitat for one," Calvin said authoritatively. "They prefer the wetlands, marshes, bogs, quagmires — you name it."

"You're talking about the black mamba — the poisonous snake, right? Have you ever seen one?"

"Not frequently. They're very elusive," Calvin said, "thus the name the elusive black mamba."

"Since mambas are native to Africa, I'd say they're very elusive in this part of the world. How did you even get up here?"

"We hiked."

"From the road? That's nearly three miles."

"There's nothing wrong with a brisk walk first thing in the morning," Calvin said. "Gets the blood pumping."

"Look, you can't just go traipsing around in these woods like this," the man said. "We found a naked dead guy in the lake just last month."

"We're not planning on going in the lake," Calvin said. "Now, if you'll excuse us—"

"Not so fast," the ranger said. "I'm going to have to call this in."

The ranger stepped away from Andy and Calvin and took out his phone. After a moment, he looked over his shoulder and said, "Yep, it's them all right."

Finished, he put away his phone and came back. "You wouldn't happen to be Calvin Alexander, would you?"

"As a matter of fact, I am," Calvin said. "I see my fame precedes me."

"Not quite," the ranger said. "A couple named Jack and Gloria Martin called the police to say you disappeared with their son Andrew." Looking at Andy, "I guess that's you."

"Yes sir," Andy said.

"A simple misunderstanding," Calvin said. "I'm positive I left them a note."

"Right. At any rate, they want him back, so I'm going to have to ask you both to come with me."

They were taken to the main ranger station. When Andy's father got there, he was furious.

"I'll take my son," Jack said, pointing at Andy. "As far as I'm concerned, you can dump this one in the lake, with or without clothes."

"Oh, come on, Jack, the boy's in perfect condition," Calvin said. "I'd never take him someplace truly dangerous."

"Dangerous?" Jack said. "They found a naked dead guy out there."

"And if I'd seen any dead naked men running or swimming around, I'd have gotten the boy out of there."

Jack grabbed Calvin by the arm and dragged him into a side room, closing the door behind them. Andy couldn't hear the conversation, but he could tell they were having a very heated discussion. After several minutes, they emerged, and Calvin seemed a bit subdued.

Jack went to his son and said, "Come on, Andy, we're getting out of here."

"What about Uncle Calvin?" Andy said.

Calvin went to Andy and bent down.

"It's okay, Andrew," Calvin said. "I just need to have a few words with the rangers. I'll be by later to get my things."

"You're leaving?" Andy said.

"You know me, always on the go," Calvin said, jostling Andy's hair. "Not to worry, I'll be in touch."

Calvin gave Andy a hug, and then Jack took Andy home.

After that, Calvin's visits became much less frequent, and he never again stayed with Andy's family when he was in town. Just before Andy headed off to college, he received a post card from Calvin that depicted the Amazon rain forest. On back was a note stating Calvin was off on a mission to look for some guy named Rockefeller. Andy lost touch with Calvin after that, but he always hoped that someday they'd link up again, so Calvin could take him to see the spitting spiders of Borneo.

The Miracle of the Magic Dollar

Carlton Drucker walked into the third-floor break room of the Atlanta offices of Bickering Plummet and approached the snack machine in the far corner. It was six-thirty in the evening and Carlton had been at his desk since seven-ten that morning, with no signs of his day ending anytime soon. Fortunately, for Carlton, the machine contained his favorite snack, the Cinnamon Crumb Cake, which only made an appearance once or twice a year, so Carlton drew some consolation from that.

The Crumb Cakes had actually been in the machine for several days, but they had been trapped behind a gooey looking honey bun that seemed well past its expiration date, and Carlton had not wanted to purchase such a disgusting looking item just to free them. At last, a secretary from the fifth floor, who was trying to purchase potato chips, accidentally keyed in the wrong number and liberated the Crumb Cakes, so Carlton had been enjoying them ever since. Carlton was certain he was the only one in the office who ate them, and his suspicions were borne out by the fact that every day the number had not decreased from the last time Carlton purchased one.

At the machine, Carlton was happy to see there were still four left, so he removed a dollar from his wallet and put it in the slot. The machine whirred and dropped his selection but then, rather than giving Carlton his change, the machine spit out the dollar he'd put in. Carlton was taken aback by what had just happened and contemplated his next move very carefully. Assured in the reality of what he had just experienced, he put the dollar back into the machine and requested another Crumb Cake. Once again, the machine made its whirring noise as it dispensed his selection and once again, it spit out the dollar, rather than giving him change.

Overcome with awe, he immediately stepped away from the machine and considered removing his shoes, because he decided that the ground upon which he was standing just might be holy. Carlton had never been a religious man, but he was convinced that he was now in the presence of some sort of higher power. He performed the miracle twice more, securing the remaining Crumb Cakes, then gathered his manna from heaven and took them to his desk.

After safely storing the goods in one of his drawers, he casually strolled over to the cubicle of his coworker Barton Esposito and leaned in.

"What's up?" Bart said, without looking at Carlton, exhibiting the effects of a long stressful day in front of his computer terminal.

"Go into the break room, put a dollar in the snack machine, and make a selection," Carlton said.

"Why?" Bart said, in a voice that suggested he was in no mood for foolishness.

"Just do it. You'll figure it out."

Carlton returned to his desk as Bart rose and headed toward the break room. Several minutes elapsed, before Bart appeared at Carlton's cube, wearing a wide grin, and holding several packages of chips and crackers.

"Man, that's cool!"

"I knew you'd think so," Carlton said.

"What do you think is causing it?"

Carlton pondered the question a moment, and then shook his head. "It's probably just out of change, but I choose to see it as a miracle from the lord."

"Are you serious?"

"No, but to think otherwise means we'd have to report it," Carlton replied.

"Good point," Bart said before returning to his desk. Holding his hands aloft, he proclaimed, "Praise be to the lord!"

For the next several days, Carlton and Bart dwelt in the land of plenty, and whenever someone would approach either of them for change to use in the machine, they gladly complied, not wanting to give away the sacred knowledge to which they'd been entrusted.

Finally, one afternoon, as they were in the break room contemplating what they wanted from the nearly empty machine, Rose Wagner, the facilities manager, came in to purchase something.

"You guys actually going to get something or are you just window shopping?" she said as she stepped past them.

"Need some change?" Bart spoke up quickly, as Rose took a dollar from her pocket.

"Why? I'll just use a dollar."

Before either man could intervene, Rose had deposited her dollar and selected the numbers corresponding to the Sour Apple Twizzlers. Just as always, after dispensing the item, the machine returned the dollar to her.

"Did you see that?" she said, holding the dollar up.

"See what?" Carlton said, looking away from her.

"I put in a dollar and the machine spit it back out," Rose responded.

"I didn't see anything," Bart said.

Carlton shrugged. "Me neither."

"That's a load of crap," Rose replied. "You were both standing right here."

Carlton stepped forward and confronted her. "We choose to see this as a miracle from the lord — the miracle of the magic dollar. You don't question miracles; you just rejoice in them, as I'm sure it says, somewhere in the Bible."

Rose put her hands on her hips and tilted her head.

"This isn't a miracle," Rose said, "the machine's malfunctioning."

"The effect is miraculous regardless of the cause," Carlton said. "I refuse to question the vessel through which the lord makes his presence known."

"How long has it been doing this?" she asked Bart.

"I don't know what you're talking about," he replied.

"Guys, this should have been reported," Rose told them. "This is someone's livelihood, you know."

Bart leaned toward Rose and spoke in a confidential tone. "Look, I understand that when stuff like this happens, the snack guy gets ripped off, but seriously, eighty cents for Cheez-Its? Even in the wide world of overpriced vending food, that's excessive."

Rose considered this. "Yeah, you've got a point. I mean, I can get these Twizzlers at Costco for about twenty cents a pack. There's the distribution angle and all, but still that's a pretty hefty markup."

"Besides, this machine has ripped me off plenty of times, and I rarely complain about it," Carlton said. "The way I see it, this just evens it all out."

Rose shook her head. "I'll give you until the end of the week, but if no one else calls this in, I'll have to. It's my job, you know?"

"Bless you, sister," Bart said, making an attempt at the sign of the cross in front of her.

"Cut it out," Rose said and walked away from them. "Close of business Friday, got it?"

The following Monday, the vending guy returned and fixed whatever it was that had been causing the machine to dispense the dollars. Carlton watched in silent resignation as the vendor restocked the shelves.

"Hey, buddy," the vendor said in a cheery tone. "Got any requests?"

"What about the Cinnamon Crumb Cakes?" Carlton asked.

The vendor shook his head. "Sorry guy, they've been discontinued. They weren't very popular, from what I hear. Strange, because they always sell out at this location."

Carlton nodded and headed over to Bart's cubicle.

"Is it done?" Bart asked, to which Carlton nodded.

"Let us not lament that which is past," Carlton replied in the cadence of a preacher. "Rather let us take solace in knowing that for a brief moment, we were in the presence of something greater than ourselves. That's something we can tell our kids one day."

Bart thought about it, and said, "I don't have any kids."

"You know what I mean," Carlton replied.

"Amen, brother."

Cheese Toast

My collection of essays, *The Cheese Toast Project*, was published 2015, including essays originally posted on my blog. One essay, *The Tragedy of Juliet*, was published in *Killing Babies* in 2016 as *Not a Love Song*, but was a better fit with the Shakespeare essays of Cheese Toast.

The Cheese Toast Project

A few years ago, I set up a photo album on Facebook called The Cheese Toast Project. On its surface, it appeared to be little more than photos of cheese toast I'd had for breakfast each morning, but my intent was for it to be an experiment in language. Specifically, I wanted to demonstrate the limitations of language in conveying an idea and used "cheese toast" as my illustration. Almost everyone understands the concept, but simply requesting a slice of cheese toast can lead to many different outcomes, depending on how one defines "cheese", "bread", and "toast".

Most will agree, that to create a slice of cheese toast, one starts with bread, then adds some sort of cheese to it, and then puts it all into a toaster for a given amount of time. Nothing could be simpler — until one considers the many types of bread, the vast array of cheeses, and the varied notions of what constitutes "toast". For instance, a slice of cheese toast could consist of Wonder Bread with Velveeta; or wheat bread with crumpled Gorgonzola; or rye bread with Swiss cheese; or a pita with grated Parmesan.

It would seem, then, that to successfully comply with someone's request for a slice of cheese toast, both parties must come to an agreement on the terms, "cheese" and "bread." The process is further complicated by the different ways one can make toast. For some, "toast" is simply a slice of bread browned in some type of oven. For others, making toast means adding margarine or butter, herbs and/or spices, and sometimes even onions, tomatoes, or mushrooms. Task a group of individuals with making a slice of cheese toast, and one could end up with as many varieties as there are people in the group, provided they have the necessary resources.

Thus, we have the disparity between general concept and specific execution. Almost anyone asked to prepare a slice of cheese toast can certainly comply with the request, but will the result be what the person making the request really wants? Would cottage cheese on a toasted baguette qualify? Cream cheese on a bagel contains the basic elements of cheese and toasted bread, but most don't refer to that as cheese toast. While there may exist a consensus on what isn't cheese toast, that doesn't bring us closer to knowing exactly what an individual's specific definition is.

Expanding on that notion, how can we be certain what some-one means when that person says "car", or "house", or "dog"? While there are commonly agreed upon generalities, there is a vast difference between a Honda Civic and a Lamborghini; a cabin and a mansion; or a Chihuahua and a Doberman. Person-al experience goes a long way toward determining the mental picture one draws when hearing each term. Just imagine the problems that can arise when one person's definition of "large" or "warm" doesn't match that of another.

This is a limitation of language. Most regard it as the single factor that separates humans from other inhabitants of the earth, but when a concept as simple as "cheese toast" can yield such a wide variety of examples, what hope does that give for conveying more abstract notions, such as love, truth, or beauty. Perhaps the genius of language is that it allows us to share ideas without fully comprehending what each other is actually saying.

In the exacting field of science, definitions are very important and usually agreed upon from the beginning. In the absence of a common frame of reference, the rest of us can only hope we'll be understood. Problems can arise when one assumes an under-standing has been reached, such as when telling someone, "You know what must be done".

The ability to communicate ideas has yielded amazing ad-vancements for the human race, but it can also be an impedi-ment when people fail to agree on basic definitions for common concepts. We should never simply assume we're being under-stood when language provides us with a mechanism for clari-fication. Whether insisting on rights and privileges, instructing someone on proper behavior, or simply asking for some cheese toast, it helps to be certain we're conveying what we truly mean, rather than assuming we're all speaking the same language, even when we are.

Failing to Succeed

I have a saying, "Hank Aaron didn't hit a home run every time." It's my way of reminding myself that for every success, there are a thousand less than perfect outcomes. In fact, failure is much more common than success. The term "trial and error" best sums up the practice of implementing a strategy, observing the positive and negative effects, and modifying procedures until the desired results are achieved. The founders of the United States didn't get things right the first time with the Articles of Confederation, and it took a Civil War to work out issues left over from ratifying the Constitution.

It has been said that one learns more from failure than success. This is because one learns from failure, versus getting something right the first time. Failure causes one to evaluate what went wrong, to examine the process and make improvements, and to "try harder" on the next attempt. In the process the brain gets rewired, and changes in attitude and behavior happen that can't be reversed. One who succeeds without much effort or "coasts" on talent alone is no better or worse for the experience. The person who fails a time or two (or more) and modifies the approach at each try, becomes more knowledgeable and better skilled. Orson Welles, in his Hollywood debut, produced what has been heralded as the greatest movie ever filmed, and never fully lived up to his potential again. Lasting success often comes to those not immediately appreciated for their talents.

George Washington wasn't highly regarded by his superiors as a young officer in the Colonial militia, and as a general, his favorite tactic was strategic retreat. Van Gogh never sold a painting in his lifetime, but, fortunately, didn't let that stifle his creativity. Penicillin came about because Alexander Fleming used a petri dish contaminated with mold spores. Joanne Rowling was a recently divorced single mother with serious financial problems, who spent her free time in a coffee shop working on the draft of what would become the first Harry Potter novel. Failure and the disappointment that comes with it often makes eventual success all the more rewarding.

The book *Rejection* by John White chronicles numerous instances where authors, filmmakers, and other public figures have endured times when their work was not recognized by critics, publishers, or the public at large. In one instance, a poet, Lee Pennington, submitted a work to a magazine and was told it was "the worst poem in the English language". Undaunted, he submitted it to another magazine, which published it and named it best poem of the year. Learning to deal with disappointment is the most important lesson one can learn, because we're more likely to be disappointed than satisfied. Accepting that failure is not the end of the world is often the first step in becoming a success.

That being said, it is, by no means easy to deal with failure, and the grander the scale, the more difficult it becomes to overcome the feelings that go with it. There is a tendency among people to personalize every interaction. Often times, when something negative happens to someone, the first instinct is for the person to wonder what he or she did to cause it. Usually, such feelings have little basis in reality. When we fail, it's always a challenge to keep believing we're capable of accomplishing the task at hand, but those who best overcome failure are the ones best positioned to succeed.

Sometimes, failure does result from individual limitations. A person with no athletic ability is not very likely to become a world-class tennis or soccer star, regardless of how much effort goes into the pursuit. Everyone has talent in some form or another, however, and sometimes it's just a matter of recognizing and nurturing it. James Boswell, biographer of Dr. Samuel Johnson, had a gift for bringing interesting people together and chronicling what happened afterward. Learning to be resourceful in the face of defeat gives one the potential to eventually succeed. We're always going to have difficulties. It's how we face them that makes all the difference.

Rise of the Know Nothings

The founders of this country were some of the most educated and enlightened individuals of their day, albeit from the privileged classes, but still they understood the value of knowledge, which is why so many of them opposed letting black slaves learn to read and write. The so-called "Greatest Generation of Americans" took advantage of educational opportunities afforded by the GI Bill after World War II to acquire the skills and knowledge needed to turn the United States into a global super power. One could argue that, despite the cost, more people attend college nowadays than at any time in the nation's history. Despite this, many people in the United States exhibit a dangerous bias toward experts.

The more educated and informed one is, the less likely one is to be trusted in this country. We see evidence of this in schools, in business, and most particularly in politics. The newcomer, uncompromising and untainted by years of corruption or back room deal making, always carries much weight with the electorate despite demonstrating no competence for the job being sought. Ironically, this negative attitude toward knowledge runs counter to the dreams of many parents who want their children to have a good education and to benefit from learning opportunities denied to those who came before them.

The media contributes quite a bit to this trend. Educated people are portrayed as nerds, awkward, socially inept, and the constant target of bullies, while shows which cater to the lowest common denominator of voyeurism regularly command high ratings. We're bombarded day in and day out with messages that school is boring and those who take their studies seriously are losers. Politicians on both sides of the aisle decry the decline in learning, all the while cutting funding for schools, vilifying teachers, and increasing the amount of paperwork and bureaucracy involved in getting the job done. Testing becomes the priority, as rote memorization of facts overrides a true appreciation of the material. Learning how to color within the lines and blindly follow instructions replaces critical thinking. Social conservatives insist on confusing scientific theory with religious dogma, while liberals insist on giving equal weight to every point of view regardless of how obscure or unrealistic some are, or how much time and effort is wasted by the pursuit.

Nihilism, defined as a systematic denial of the reality of experience, has become the guiding philosophy for many Americans. While it is possible to have knowledge without wisdom, or vice versa, when knowledge and wisdom are combined, the result is a better-rounded individual and a more dynamic society. Concerted efforts to encourage students to pursue science and math in high school and college led the United States to the moon, and fueled the rapid technological growth seen in the latter half of the twentieth century. This should convince us that when education is given its proper place in society, everyone benefits.

Education is the greatest equalizer among people. When one is given access to a good formal education, one is free to chart his or her course in life. Strong public schools always coincide with growing societies. Before the time public schools became the norm, motivated individuals went to great lengths to secure the means for a quality education as a guaranteed route to prosperity and success. Some of history's greatest individuals arose from humble roots by sheer determination, and education was the tool that facilitated their rise. We need to once again place learning into a position of prominence in this society and begin to see education as a fundamental right for all and experience as a desirable trait that contributes to the health and happiness of the nation.

Strange Bedfellows

The problem with our current system of governance is that it takes so long and costs so much to gain and retain office, that only someone comfortably wealthy or in the pocket of wealthy business interests can afford to run. Factored into the equation is the tremendous amount of scrutiny to which most public figures — in particular candidates — are subjected and the enormous number of hoops through which one must jump to prove oneself worthy of high office. Oftentimes the election isn't won by the best candidate but by the candidate who's most determined to get elected. In addition, the corrupting influence of power and money can turn even the most altruistic of individuals totally against the ideals that caused him or her to run for office in the first place.

The situation in the U.S. is compounded by what I call "two-party tyranny", or the belief fostered by the major political parties that only the Democrats or the Republicans are qualified to govern and that independent candidates have no chance of winning. This is due, in part to the actions of politicians of both stripes crafting the laws that keep them in office to the exclusion of all others. It is nearly impossible for a candidate to be elected above the local level without belonging to one party or the other. The news media is very much in active collusion by choosing to ignore or belittle candidates not of the major parties, thereby undermining the credibility of independent or viable alternate party candidates. Since most debates are arranged by the media in conjunction with the major parties, it becomes even more difficult for candidates outside the mainstream to participate in the process.

Changing the system takes time and patience, but most of all, relentless determination, and most people simply give up after repeated setbacks. The religious right, on the other hand, rode a single issue, abortion, into control of one of the two major political parties in this country. Now, if we don't like what the Democrats have to offer, our only option is to turn the government over to a group of religious extremists, whose only solutions to all social problems are to lower taxes and re-institute prayer in schools, all the while vilifying homosexuals, and interfering with the reproductive freedom of women. For those who don't like that, we're left with a party run by a bunch of weak-willed corporate shills who make no moves without consulting the latest opinion poll. Given these options the question isn't why so few people vote, but why anyone bothers to vote at all.

This is not to say that there aren't good people on both sides who sincerely want to make a difference and who view politics as a means toward that end, but their voices are increasingly drowned out by the endless drone of useless political theater which substitutes for intelligent discourse in the media. The best way to be noticed is to be totally outrageous, regardless of how abhorrent ones' ideas are when presented. The success of a particularly odious candidate in the 2016 presidential race showed how cynical and self-serving the process has become. When one isn't certain if he or she is watching Jerry Springer or the latest partisan debate for high office, the problem becomes all too clear.

The situation has gotten so bad that our elected representatives at the national level are completely at a loss as to how to carry out the jobs they were elected to perform. They spend so much time and effort trying to gain and retain power that they've lost sight of the fact that campaigning for office is not the job they were sent to Washington to accomplish. At best, they spend three months at work and the rest of their time is spent raising money and bashing their political opponents. The only thing worse is when they do show up for work and pass legislation that curtails another of our freedoms, or waste time and taxpayer funds conducting hearings aimed at hurting the opposition solely for political gain.

Ultimately, the solution rests with the electorate. When we point the finger of blame, we need to begin with ourselves, because we've allowed the situation to get so far out of hand by not taking the process seriously. The 2018 mid-term election has shown that Democracy starts with local action. Find good people, encourage them to run for office, support them, and, above all, insist on transparency and accountability from them. The electorate in this country has abdicated its responsibility to hold our representatives accountable for their decisions, and the professional politicians in charge of the system know this. Is there any wonder they feel no need whatsoever to account for their activities?

If one's representative to Congress only moved to the region shortly before the election and spends most of his or her time outside the district, how can that person be expected to know what's best for the constituency he or she is supposed to serve?

Scenarios like this happen again and again in U.S. elections and apathetic citizens simply let it happen, then spend the duration between elections complaining about how bad things are.

Most people in the U.S. behave as though politics is just something that happens to someone else. They believe the political system is rigged and there is nothing anyone can do to fix it. While I agree the system is rigged, I do believe there's something we can do about it, though it won't be easy or quick. The system we're dealing with in the U.S. didn't spring up overnight, and outside of complete overthrow, which usually causes more problems than it solves, it won't be fixed in one fell swoop. Still, I believe we should try, otherwise we'll become increasingly disconnected to a system which, despite all its problems, still makes vital decisions which have a huge impact on the quality of the lives we lead.

The first step is to be informed. We live in an age where a massive amount of information is at our fingertips. The White House, Congress and Supreme Court, not to mention most state legislatures and local governments have all their votes, rulings and dispatches online. Most members of Congress have sites where they publish news and official information about their activities in Washington, their voting records, and contact information both locally and in the capitol. If an important vote is held and one's representative in Congress isn't there due to a political fundraiser or other less important speaking engagement, the constituents deserve to know why that was deemed more important than serving the needs of those being represented. Equally, if one's representative votes for legislation that has a damaging impact on his or her home region or against a bill that would have benefited the folks back home, the citizens have a right to ask why and change representation at the first opportunity if not satisfied with the answer. We voted them in, and we can vote them out.

Of course, building a new system would take decades, starting from scratch, and reforming the current system might take just as long. From FDR's New Deal to LBJ's Great Society was a span of thirty to forty years. The conservative movement now controlling the Republican Party started while I was in college thirty years ago. Most political movements begin in reaction to what's happening in the country at a given time and take hold gradually. Often, by the time its leaders finally attain power, society has begun to swing back in the other direction. Politics can change in a revolution, but it's more likely to do so by evolution with smaller steps.

While it may, at times, seem futile to participate, it's only through such participation that things begin to improve. 2018 showed that when the electorate does bother to show up, important changes take place. It's in the politicians' best interest to keep voter turnout low. Below are a few suggestions for improving the process.

- Campaigns for office cannot start before January of the calendar year in which the election will be held.
- All campaigns will be publicly-financed and all candidates will be allotted an equal amount of money.
- No private funding will be allowed either by the candidate or outside parties.
- Debates will be managed by a non-partisan organization which will select the venue, moderators, and agenda, and will arrange all media coverage.
- Any eligible candidate may participate in the election regardless of personal beliefs, political affiliations, or background in office.
- All candidates receive the same treatment, consideration, and scrutiny from the media.
- A primary will be held sometime between May and July in which any qualified candidate may run for any available office; the top four vote getters in each race proceed to the general election in November.
- Congressional apportionment of states following each census will be governed by a nonpartisan council comprised of individuals drafted at the city or county level and using the latest technology to insure a fair distribution of voters.
- Campaign ads must deal with the issues and refrain from personal attacks or ads which disparage another candidate.

Assassins from the Future

While it cannot be definitively proven that the future has already happened, we can be certain that the future will become the present at some point, and with the phenomenal advances in technology seen throughout the twentieth and into the twenty-first century, a day may well arrive when humans will discover ways to travel backward in time. For this reason, it is advisable that people in this day and age begin preparing for the possibility that at some point after time travel has been perfected, someone with a serious grievance against a person living in the current day, might undertake to dispatch an assassin or assassins to rid the timeline of this perceived threat.

Certainly, important people, such as presidents, business leaders, and other celebrities are fair game, but average people should not rule out the impact they are having on the timeline. Actions have consequences, and one cannot know for certain what the ultimate outcome of his or her activities might be. A decision seemingly as harmless as the choice of one's daily footwear could set off ripples throughout time that could lead to disastrous consequences for some unfortunate individual in the distant future, and for this reason, it's best to be on one's guard.

One should never assume he or she is not important enough to warrant the attention of some dystopian future regime seeking to erase one's influence on history. As shown in the beloved holiday classic, *It's a Wonderful Life*, the loss of a single individual to history can have a profound and devastating impact on people with whom this individual has never even directly interacted.

A popular legend tells of a British soldier during World War I who took pity on a German corporal he found in his gun sight, sparing the man's life, and taking him prisoner instead. This corporal went on to become chancellor of Germany and initiated the Second World War. Humans are social beings and each interaction leads to further interaction, so the impact of a given life can cause ripples throughout society, affecting people far beyond the immediate scope of the individual's attention.

Despite this, one should not attempt to trick fate by being the sort of person a futuristic antagonist would not want to erase from history. Just as Oedipus's father tried to avert fate by sending his son away to die, only to have Oedipus return and carry out his preordained role, attempting to avoid a future outcome may, in fact, bring about the very outcome one is trying to avoid. One cannot be certain what will or won't cause someone distress a hundred or more years from now, prompting that person to desire one's removal from the timeline. The best advice is to live one's life as one chooses, but always be mindful of the impact one's decisions are having, while remaining on the lookout for signs that someone in the future has taken umbrage with one's actions. Even when being pursued by a futuristic assassin, one still has many advantages working in one's favor.

Take solace in the fact that it won't be easy for someone from the future to pinpoint one's location with any degree of accuracy, though social media is making it much easier for individuals to broadcast their whereabouts. We cannot be certain, though, how much of our current culture will still exist fifty to a hundred years from now. In just the span of the last twenty to thirty years, technology has rendered many permanent storage mediums obsolete, such as floppy discs and tape drives, making it all but impossible to retrieve data stored on them. Consider how difficult it is to garner details on someone living in the 1930s, even though records on individuals from that era still exist.

As pervasive as the Internet can be, unless someone makes the effort to store and catalog specific types of data, the vast amount of information available constantly dilutes the stream of posts, photos, and videos. Only a fraction of items posted to YouTube become Internet sensations, and even one's closest associates quickly lose track of the concert or theatrical review one posted to Facebook a few days ago. Still, the information exists, and an obsessive futuristic antagonist, hell bent on wreaking havoc on the timeline may well have the time, energy, and resources to pursue such goals.

One may also take comfort in the fact that superior technology may not be an advantage to an individual who has traveled back into our time. An assassin traveling to the current day from some future date will no doubt be constrained by the limitations of our technology. For instance, if one of us were somehow transported to the Civil War era with an iPhone, not only would there be no way to charge it, but the network needed to communicate using it won't exist, making it almost useless. Granted, technology from the future will undoubtedly be far advanced from ours, and the ability to establish a wireless network hub from a cellular phone already exists to some extent, but networks, and storage mediums needed to convey data and files would not be present, and it's not likely any futuristic technology would be backward compatible.

Some may point out that the ability to send a time traveler to a specific place and time may be sketchy, but we should not be lulled into a false sense of security by our lack of knowledge as to how time travel might work. One should assume that a society capable of sending people backward in time would have worked out most of the kinks before offering it to the sort of people likely to want to alter the timeline. Still, we can assume that people won't just be popping in from out of nowhere, regardless of who may be present to witness the arrival. The key element of sending an assassin from the future will be surprise, so someone just arriving in a flash of light is certain to cause a few alarms to go off. Given that it's not likely a two-way portal will exist, at least until enough travelers have arrived to construct one, the time traveler will most likely be resigned to the notion that it's a one-way trip and may not be fully motivated to carry out the assignment.

It is imperative that if one believes he or she is being pursued by a futuristic assassin, this information should not be shared with anyone. It's not likely one's friends or relatives would believe such a claim in the first place, and would view it as a joke, or perhaps a sign of mental illness. Equally so, one should not directly confront a suspected futuristic assassin, not least of which because it could lead to the individual hastening his or her plans to eradicate the target. It is highly unlikely such an individual would freely admit being an assassin from the future and could use the accusation to call into question one's mental state, leading to incarceration, and making one much more easy to find and kill. The best course of action is to remain calm and look for telltale signs to confirm one is, in fact, in the presence of someone from the future.

Be alert! Assassins from the future are nothing if not wily. It won't be easy to trick one into showing his or her hand. Diligence is very important. Does this individual seem overly nostalgic for modern day cars, or buildings recently constructed, as though recalling them from memory? Has this individual shown little or no surprise over catastrophic events that have occurred, as though these events were anticipated? Does this person display far too much confidence in making predictions on current sporting events, as though the outcome is a foregone conclusion? The devil is in the details, and even the most astute futuristic assassin could have quirks which give away the game.

Listen for odd turns of phrase, strange patterns of speech, or unfamiliarity with common clichés or sayings. Does this individual render a blank stare when confronted with the names or actions of well-known performers, or sports figures? Certainly, there are those in the current day who don't follow the antics of the Real Housewives or denizens of the Jersey Shore, but enough unfamiliarity with common culture could be just the warning one needs to spot someone not from our time.

An assassin from the future will want to be discrete. It's not likely such a person would zap someone with a laser, or otherwise employ technology not found in our time. Futuristic assassins must be resourceful and will go out of their way to not draw attention to themselves. These factors can be used to one's advantage in attempting to uncover a futuristic threat. One strategy would be to somehow discretely convey to the individual that one is aware of his or her intentions, which may not avert the danger, but might cause the individual to strike out rashly, after which retaliatory measures would be justified.

A word of caution must be inserted here. One should not assume every individual one suspects of being from the future is here to cause someone harm. Perhaps the individual has a personal reason for employing time travel, to right a wrong, visit a deceased family member, or prevent some tragedy from happening. It's entirely possible that the person one suspects of plotting against one's life is merely here to take advantage of a fluctuation in the stock market or get in on the ground floor of a lucrative business. If the suspected time traveler shows no particular interest in one's day to day schedule, cannot be found hanging about one's cubicle at work for no reason, or otherwise exhibits no overt concerns about one's whereabouts or activities, it's entirely likely this individual is simply enjoying the fruits of being able to visit different times and presents no immediate danger.

It is hoped that these guidelines will be of assistance to anyone suspecting incursions from generations yet to be. Most of us, may never have to deal with visitors from the future, but it pays to be ready just in case. We can't count on every futuristic assassin being a relentless, unfeeling cyborg, or otherwise exhibiting signs easily detected. By observing these guidelines, one can be confident of remaining in the timeline, regardless of how persistent some futuristic denizen is to prevent it.

A Soldier's Story

On the freezing morning of Sunday, 29 November 1863, Union soldiers defending Fort Sanders in Knoxville, Tennessee leveled their rifles at advancing Confederate soldiers and fired, killing or wounding more than eight hundred. Among those killed was Nathaniel G. Lupo, my great-great-grandfather. He might have died from a single shot, a barrage of bullets, or a mortar blast. He may have been tripping over the baling wire that had been strung between tree stumps to slow down any assault, attempting to scale the frozen wall of the fort with a stand of colors, or struggling in the ditch surrounding the fort, while above, Union gunners rained down bullets on him and his comrades. The exact circumstances of his final moments have been lost to history, though one can be certain they were chaotic, and undoubtedly horrifying. The poorly planned assault on Fort Sanders, carried out by troops serving in the First Corps of the Army of Northern Virginia under James Longstreet, lasted approximately twenty minutes and gained absolutely nothing for the Confederate cause.

My grandfather lived with my family when I was a child and died when I was ten, but I knew my great-uncle reasonably well. Unfortunately, my interest in the history of our family had not yet manifested itself, and by the time I started asking questions, neither of them, nor my great-aunt, were around to supply any answers. My father claimed to know very little about his ancestors, but if I asked him specific questions, such as whether or not his great-grandfather fought and died in the Civil War, he usually knew the answer. *The Roster of the Confederate Soldiers of Georgia*, compiled by Lillian Henderson, lists four Lupos who fought in the war for Georgia, two brothers, one close cousin, and one distant cousin.

What I know of Nathaniel mainly comes from the few official records he left behind. Given his age on the census in 1850 and 1860, he appears to have been born around 1835, most likely in Houston County, Georgia. On the 1850 census, he's living in the household of Robert D. Sinclair, a physician and large landowner in Dooly County, Georgia. On 2 November 1854, he married Sarah Amanda Cone, and by 1860, Nathaniel, his father David, and uncle Giles, with their families, had moved to Jackson County, Florida.

A letter from David Lupo, dated 1 April 1860, mentions Nathaniel, and reports the activity surrounding their farm. Nathaniel and Amanda had three children listed in their household in 1860, Nancy T, age 5, William, age 3, and my great-grandfather, James David, who was about eight months old. There is a story in my family, told to me by one of my father's first cousins, that Nathaniel was a fiddle player, which would be interesting, considering his ancestors were as well, but I have found no contemporary sources with which to confirm this.

In 1861, Nathaniel and his family apparently returned to Dooly County, where on 22 June 1861, he enlisted for service in the Georgia Volunteer Infantry. His company, dubbed "The Dooly Light Infantry" and headed by Captain Joseph Armstrong, was sent to Cobb County for training, and later to Virginia, where they became Company I in the 18th Georgia Regiment, which was initially part of John Bell Hood's "Texas" brigade. In 1864, Hood would be the general who surrendered Atlanta to Sherman, but in 1861-62 the youthful Hood was just establishing his reputation for being a fierce and reckless commander. His Texas brigade, including the 18th Georgia, was responsible for breaking the Union line at Gaines Mill, and turning the tide in the Seven Days campaign, where Lee drove McClellan from Virginia. In his memoirs, Hood referred to the 18th as "bold and trusty" and regretted the loss of the troop in the reorganization following the Seven Days campaign.

The battle-hardened 18th Georgia was transferred to Thomas R. R. Cobb's Georgia brigade (later led by William Tatum Wofford), where they continued to be a part of the shock troops, first in, last out, in many of the battles in which they participated. The 18th Georgia played a decisive role at Second Manassas, fought at Antietam — the bloodiest single day in United States history — and was stationed behind the Stone Wall on Marye's Heights at Fredericksburg, which was an absolute bloodbath for Union troops attempting to take the position. The First Corps under James Longstreet participated during the second day's fighting at Gettysburg, with the 18th Georgia heavily engaged in the Peach Orchard. Records show that shortly after the Battle of Gettysburg, Nathaniel was admitted to the hospital in Virginia, but the cause isn't given.

In short, Nathaniel didn't just serve in the war, he was front and center at some of the bloodiest and most brutal fighting of the deadliest war in United States history. Having never served in combat myself, I cannot begin to comprehend what participating in such carnage can do to a person's psyche. Records show, in addition to the aftermath of Gettysburg, Nathaniel spent time in hospitals following several battles, including Antietam, without the cause being reported. The 18th Georgia was among the troops who accompanied Longstreet on detached service in Tennessee and Georgia in fall and winter of 1863, though the 18th did not participate in the Battle of Chickamauga, the one battle the First Corps fought on Georgia soil. Longstreet didn't get along very well with Braxton Bragg, who was in command of forces around Chattanooga, and left to conduct independent operations in Eastern Tennessee, which brought the First Corps to the outskirts of Knoxville by early November.

Surviving accounts of the battle in which Nathaniel lost his life are marred by the fact that in the aftermath of the assault, Longstreet brought charges against several of his subordinates, including Major General Lafayette McLaws, who was in command of the division which included the 18th Georgia. Longstreet accused McLaws of not providing proper equipment to carry out the assault, while McLaws pointed the finger at Longstreet for providing him with faulty reconnaissance. The main point of contention appears to center around how much of an obstacle the ditch surrounding the fort would be, and McLaws stated he was assured by Colonel E. P. Alexander, artillery commander and a military engineer, and by Longstreet himself that they had witnessed a soldier crossing the ditch without difficulty at the point where the attack was to occur. McLaws confirmed that the majority of soldiers who died were killed in the ditch.

A report by opposing General Ambrose Burnside, stated that casualties were left in the ditch overnight in freezing conditions, with the wounded calling out for help. The following morning, Burnside mercifully proposed a truce, which Longstreet accepted, allowing the Confederates to tend to their wounded and bury their dead. Burnside reported that ninety-two bodies were turned over to the Confederates. Nathaniel was most likely among them.

In all probability, I would not be here had Nathaniel lived, given that his death is the main event which started my family on their journey through the next century. Nathaniel's actions, returning to Georgia, and enlisting for service, probably felt obvious to him. He may have believed he had no choice in the matter, yet every step of the way, he made the choices, up to and including where he stood in formation in preparation for the assault on the fort on 29 November. Just as I do not know the exact circumstances of his death, I also do not know what became of his body. In all likelihood, he was buried in a mass grave on the battlefield and left behind as the army moved on.

His name does not appear among those re-interred in the city cemetery after the battle, though recently, the grave of his commanding officer, Solon Z. Ruff, has been located and marked in Knoxville, by the Sons of Confederate Veterans. Reports of the battle indicate Ruff died in the ditch surrounding the fort while cheering on his men, and since he was commanding Wofford's Brigade, that's most likely where Nathaniel died as well.

Most of current day Knoxville, and the University of Tennessee at Knoxville, were built over top of the battlefield. In 1982, I went there with two friends to attend the World's Fair, with no idea of the importance the city had in my family's history. While I'm not a believer in signs, I will report that the first day we were there, it rained the entire time.

One cannot speak of Confederate ancestors without invoking the memory of the cause for which they fought. Let me be clear, I do not honor the Confederacy as a governmental entity, nor do I believe in what the politicians of the Southern states attempted to accomplish by breaking away from the Union. Secession was a horrible idea in 1860, and those in the South who invoke the specter of secession for their own political ends today, merely perpetuate the arrogance and ignorance of those who led the South to secede, leading to tens of thousands of needless deaths in the resulting conflict.

Since the end of the war, states which made up the Confederacy have attempted, and largely succeeded, in changing public perceptions about the war, shifting the cause from slavery to states' rights. None of this matters. We don't need to speculate on why Georgia seceded because the people who made the decision to secede spelled out in fairly clear terms why they were doing it.

Georgia's Declaration of Secession (approved 29 January 1861) gives a comprehensive outline of the animosities between slave states and those who would abolish slavery, in particular:

> *"The party of Lincoln, called the Republican party, under its present name and organization...* While it attracts to itself by its creed the scattered advocates of exploded political heresies, of condemned theories in political economy, the advocates of commercial restrictions, of protection, of special

privileges, of waste and corruption in the administration of Government, anti-slavery is its mission and its purpose... *The question of slavery was the great difficulty in the way of the formation of the Constitution.*

"*An anti-slavery party must necessarily look to the North alone for support...* The feeling of anti-slavery, which it was well known was very general among the people of the North, had been long dormant or passive; it needed only a question to arouse it into aggressive activity... *We had acquired a large territory by successful war with Mexico; Congress had to govern it; how, in relation to slavery, was the question then demanding solution. This state of facts gave form and shape to the anti-slavery sentiment throughout the North and the conflict began...*

"The Constitution declares that persons charged with crimes in one State and fleeing to another shall be delivered up on the demand of the executive authority of the State from which they may flee, to be tried in the jurisdiction where the crime was committed. It would appear difficult to employ language freer from ambiguity, yet *for above twenty years the non-slave-holding States generally have wholly refused to deliver up to us persons charged with crimes affecting slave property...*

"*A similar provision of the Constitution requires them to surrender fugitives from labor. This provision and the one last referred to were our main inducements for confederating with the Northern States. Without them it is historically true that we would have rejected the Constitution.*

"*The non-slave-holding States generally repealed all laws intended to aid the execution of that act, and imposed penalties upon those citizens whose loyalty to the Constitution and their oaths might induce them to discharge their duty. Congress then passed the act of 1850, providing for the complete execution of this duty by Federal officers...* The Supreme Court unanimously, and their own local courts with equal unanimity (with the single and temporary exception of the supreme court of Wisconsin), sustained its constitutionality in all of its provisions.

That's about as explicit as one can get on the issue. In fact, slaveholding states had called upon the United States government to nullify laws in states such as Massachusetts which prevented slave owners from reclaiming slaves who'd run away and granted freedom to any slave who happened to travel there with the slaveholder.

As to why the individual soldiers signed up, in the absence of correspondence from them, we cannot know their specific motives, but, most likely, Nathaniel, and others like him, signed up for service because he thought his home and family were threatened by a potential invasion of the state. Nathaniel returned to Georgia, volunteered for Georgia, was trained and equipped by Georgia to fight for Georgia, and instead, he and other volunteers immediately found themselves shipped out to Virginia to protect the Confederate capital, leaving Georgia's defenses in disarray.

In a dispatch to the Confederate War Department dated 11 November 1861, Georgia's governor, Joseph E. Brown, specifically requested return of three brigades including Wofford's, which comprised the 18th Georgia, because of a feared invasion by enemy forces. This wasn't a trivial matter given Georgia's extensive coastline. Dispatches show considerable apprehension among the governor and mayors of several cities of an invasion targeting Savannah, Brunswick, or Augusta. The request was denied by the Confederate war department, as were other requests by Governor Brown. At the time, there was tension but no outright hostilities in Virginia, and the 18th Georgia had been assigned to picket duty around Richmond where Nathaniel's brother-in-law William Thomas Cone was killed around the time of Governor Brown's request.

Regardless of Nathaniel's motives in taking up arms against the United States, it is pointless to ignore or downplay that aspect of my family's history, as it plays so great a part in it, just as my ancestors played their part in the history of this country. While I do not always agree with the decisions my ancestors made, I cannot deny those decisions played a part in the circumstances which eventually led to me being here. Had Nathaniel lived, he may have decided to take his family west, as many did in the wake of the war; or returned to Florida; or traveled elsewhere in Georgia. Records show that his death had a devastating effect on his young family.

Other than her listing on a record of widows who received a salt ration in 1864, no records whatsoever have been found on his widow, Amanda, until she applied for a pension with the state of Georgia in the 1890s, and the fate of their daughter, Nancy, is unknown. Their son William shows up on the incomplete census of 1870, in Dooly County, living near the family of Nelson Moye in or near Pinehurst, Georgia, and in 1880, their son David can also be found near the Moyes in Pinehurst, living away from Nathaniel's brothers and sisters in and around Vienna.

References:

Henderson, Lillian, *Roster of the Confederate Soldiers of Georgia, 1861-1865*, Georgia State Division of Confederate Pensions and Records, Longina & Porter 1960.

The War of the Rebellion: A Compilation of the Official Records of the Union and Confederate Armies, United States War Department, Government Printing Office, Washington, DC, 1880-1901.

Georgia Declaration of Secession, *Official Records of Georgia, Serial IV, Volume 1*, pp. 81-85, text found online at the website for Yale University's Law School.

The Lupos and Shakespeare

Ambrose (da Milano) Lupo was brought to England as part of an ensemble of string players around May of 1540 by Henry VIII. Some scholars believe this was in connection with Henry's marriage to Anne of Cleves, but given the timing, Ambrose and colleagues would have arrived as the marriage was breaking up, rather than being there in time to provide entertainment. Rather, Henry's decision seems to have been guided by a desire to raise the standards of English music, and the impact these musicians had would be felt for more than a century. Ambrose, sons Peter and Joseph, along with other families such as the Bassanos, the Laniers, and the Comeys, established musical dynasties that endured throughout the reign of the Tudor monarchs, and into the reign of the Stewarts, up to the establishment of the Commonwealth. Ambrose, Peter, and Joseph were among a group of musicians credited with introducing the violin to England.

Joseph first shows up in Tudor household accounts in 1566 and Peter is first listed in 1570. Before this, Peter was employed by Robert Dudley, 1st Earl of Leicester, a favorite of Queen Elizabeth. Ambrose was among the musicians who marched in the funeral procession of Henry VIII and at the coronations of Edward VI and Elizabeth I, and Peter, Joseph, and their sons, each named Thomas, marched at the funeral of Elizabeth I. Ambrose served for over fifty years, ending with his death on 10 February 1591.

By the time works attributed to Shakespeare started appearing on stages in London, Peter and Joseph would have been well established in their positions at court. Parish records show that Peter lived in the East End of London in Aldgate, near the theater district. While it's hard to say how much the musicians would have interacted with the playwright, there is evidence from Shakespeare's work that the playwright had an extensive knowledge of music and drew inspiration from the Italian musicians at court. Many of the plays are set in Northern Italian locales, such as Verona, Milan, and Padua, and the work is peppered with musical references, from the Duke in Twelfth Night proclaiming, "If music be the food of love, play on" to Hamlet admonishing Rosencrantz and Guildenstern, "Though you may fret me, you will not play upon me."

As an Italian at the English court, Peter's name was often rendered in many interesting ways. In some documents, he's listed as Peter, in others he's Petro, or Pietro. In the listing of New Year's gifts for 1585, he's identified as Petruchio Lupo. This discovery was made all the more intriguing given that, at the time, his wife's name was Katherine. Petruchio and Katherine (or Katerina) are major characters in The Taming of the Shrew. A look at other characters from this play yields more interesting parallels. In Shrew, Petruchio has a servant named Peter, a servant named Joseph, a servant named Philip, and a servant named Nicholas. "Petruchio" Lupo, better known as Peter, had a brother named Joseph, a son named Phillip, and a colleague named Nicholas Lanier, suggesting Shakespeare name-checked several musical families. The similarities extend to a second play.

Petruchio, in Shrew, claims to be the son and sole heir of Antonio, a wealthy merchant, recently deceased, from Verona. Verona is part of Veneto or Venetia which, in Shakespeare's time, was in the Republic of Venice. This suggests that Petruchio could be connected to another of Shakespeare's protagonists, Antonio, the title character from The Merchant of Venice. In that play, Antonio is the benefactor of Bassanio, and more than one scholar has noted the similarity of this character's name to the family of recorder players, the Bassanos. In Merchant, however, Antonio is presented as a bachelor without a son. Venice is notable in the history of the Italian musicians, as it was in Venice where the Lupos, Bassanos, and other musical families were recruited into royal service by Henry's agents. In Shakespeare's other play set in Verona, Romeo and Juliet, there is mention of a Petrucio as a guest at the Capulets' party, though no details are given on him.

Peter's brother, Joseph, married Laura Bassano, and Laura was cousin to Emilia or Aemilia Bassano, who married Alfonso Lanier, the brother of Nicholas. Emilia Bassano Lanier is believed by a number of scholars to have been the Dark Woman of Shakespeare's sonnets. Much of the evidence connecting Emilia to Shakespeare comes from Simon Forman, an astrologer with designs on Emilia. Forman states she was the mistress of Henry Carey, 1st Baron Hunsdon, who, as Lord Chamberlain, was the patron of Shakespeare after his relationship with Emilia had ended. The facts that can be verified about her, make Emilia an ideal candidate for the model on which Shakespeare based Katerina in Shrew, not least of which being the fact that she's the daughter of Baptiste Bassano. Baptista Minola is the name given to the father of Katerina in Shrew.

Early in the 1600s, Emilia Lanier published a volume of poetry under her own name entitled Salve Deus Rex Judaeorum (Hail, God, King of the Jews), something unheard of for a woman during this era. There are only a few known examples of women who published books during this time and Emilia was the only poet. Emilia's work spotlights a number of notable women throughout English society — many of whom she hoped to recruit as patrons — and emphasizes that women have been unfairly maligned throughout history and deserve equality and autonomy in their own right. In his work, *Shakespeare's Dark Lady*, John Hudson presents a compelling case for Emilia as a candidate in the authorship debates over who actually wrote some or all of Shakespeare's work.

Hudson lays out his case by identifying the many communities of knowledge to which the playwright would have needed to belong to include such accurate court, legal, medical, and musical references in the plays and demonstrates that Emilia indeed had such a background. Hudson highlights numerous references in the works which, he states, allude to Emilia, including the character Emilia in Othello, and Emilius and Bassianus in Titus Andronicus. If a woman was the author of some or all of Shakespeare's plays, this fact would have been erased from history, and if Emilia was that woman, it would certainly explain references to the Italians at court in the plays.

Evidence exists that the Lupos and Bassanos were Jews. Notably, Ambrose and his fellow string players appear to be among the "secret Jews" rounded up by Henry's men early in 1542 and held in the Tower for a period of time before being allowed to quietly leave England. The Spanish ambassador, Eustice Chapuys alludes to this incident in a letter to a colleague, and hints at the musical background of the prisoners, "however well they may sing, they will not be able to fly away from their cages without leaving feathers behind" and in household accounts, the string players are listed with the notation, "they be gon to their contry." Later, Ambrose shows up among records of the Inquisition in Venice, in testimony from a young singer named Orazio Cogno, identified as someone responsible for letting Orazio read material the Church deemed heretical, while Orazio was in England. More recently, a YDNA test on a direct male descendant of Ambrose shows markers in common with descendants of Jewish Diaspora groups.

The Merchant of Venice and The Taming of the Shrew are among Shakespeare's most controversial plays, Merchant for its harsh portrayal of Jews, and Shrew for its treatment of women. An important parallel can be drawn from Merchant, however, given that Shylock is a Venetian Jew forced to convert to Christianity, and the musicians, if they were Jews, had to convert, or at least pretend to convert, to avoid repercussions in a hostile society. The purpose of the Inquisition, in fact, was to ferret out Jews who held to their faith while professing Christianity in public. In Merchant, Shylock is referred to as "wolvish, bloody, starved and ravenous," recalling the words of Genesis 49:27, which describe Benjamin as a ravenous wolf. Identification with Benjamin probably led the Lupos to adopt their surname, as "Lupo" is the Italian word for "wolf" which would mean that the origin of this family's name is chronicled in Genesis.

Peter Lupo would have been in his early fifties in 1585 and in his fifties and sixties throughout much of the time the plays were being written. His identification as "Petruchio" has only been found in one place, but the fact that he's recorded as such suggests he was sometimes known by this name, perhaps among his musical colleagues. As with most writers, Shakespeare undoubtedly drew upon familiar people and situations for inspiration. Peter would have been well-known around London, given his placement at court, and he did inhabit the theater district in the city. In later life, Peter retired to Kent, where he died around 1608. His son Albiano was among the earliest settlers of Virginia in 1610, and his son Phillip, through a son by the same name, was the father of the earliest enduring branch of the Lupo family in America.

Notable Musical References in Shakespeare

Hamlet: Just after the play within a play, one of the players enters with a recorder (the Bassanos) and Hamlet tries to get Guildenstern to play it. After Guildenstern protests that he can't, Hamlet chastises him and says, "Though you may fret me, you will not play upon me." "Fret" refers to the viols (the Lupos), which were fretted instruments played with a bow. In depictions I've seen, the larger ones look like guitars, but the player is seated with the instrument on his lap and playing it with a bow instead of strumming the strings.

Twelfth Night: In describing Sir Andrew Aguecheek, Toby Belch says, "he plays o' the viol-de-gamboys (viola da gambas), and speaks three or four languages word for word without book" which could easily describe the Lupos and other viol players, who probably spoke the languages of the countries in which they had resided including Italy (Italian), Belgium (French and Flemish), and possibly Amsterdam (Dutch). If the Lupos originated in Spain, they may have also spoken Spanish and Ladino, which was the language spoken by Sephardic Jews. I have copies of two letters written by Peter Lupo, probably dictated to a scribe, who wrote down a rough mix of Italian, Spanish and Latin.

Romeo and Juliet: When Tybalt approaches Mercutio before they fight, he says Mercutio "consorts" with Romeo. "Consort" was a term used when two or more musical groups performed together, like the viols and recorders sometimes did. Mercutio takes issue with the word "consort" and draws a comparison between dance and combat, then removes his sword and says, "Here's my fiddlestick," a reference to the fiddles or viols, which were played at dances. Consorts in English music of the Tudor era were forerunners of the modern symphony orchestra.

References

Ashbee, Andrew, Records of English Court Music, Vol. VI, 1558-1603, Aldershot, England, Scolar Press, 1992.

Holman, Peter, Four and Twenty Fiddlers: The Violin at the English Court 1540-1690, New York, Oxford University Press, 1993.

Holman, Peter, "The English Royal Violin Consort in the Sixteenth Century", Proceedings of the Royal Musical Association, Vol. 109 (1982/83).

Prior, Roger, "Jewish Musicians at the Tudor Court", The Musical Quarterly, Vol. 69 (1983).

Prior, Roger, "A second Jewish community in Tudor London", Jewish Historical Studies, Transactions of the Jewish Historical Society of England, Volume XXXI (1988-90).

Prior, Roger, "More Light on the Dark Lady", Financial Times, October 10, 1987.

Letters and Papers, Foreign and Domestic of the Reign of Henry VIII, Vol. XVII, 1542, Printed for Her Majesty's Stationery Office by the "Norfolk Chronicle" Company, Ltd., Norwich, London, 1900.

Testimony of Orazio Cogno before the Venice Inquisition on August 27th, 1577, The Ever Reader, Number 5, Spring/Summer 1997.

Hudson, John, Shakespeare's Dark Lady, Amelia Bassano Lanier: The Woman Behind Shakespeare's Plays? Gloucestershire, Amberley Publishing, 2014.

Simon Forman Casebooks, project at Cambridge University, Cambridge, UK (casebooks.lib.cam.ac.uk/reading-the-casebooks/who-were-the-practitioners/simon-forman).

Listen to the Warm

When I was a teenager, I had very specific ideas about what constituted poetry, rhyming verses, measured lines, lofty subjects like love and death. Then I read *Listen to the Warm* by Rod McKuen, and everything changed. I was aware of McKuen's work as a singer and songwriter, having seen him on television in the 70s, and heard recordings of his on the radio, but I was not as familiar with his published poetry. I ran across the book in the East Point branch of the Fulton County public library, and the name recognition caused me to borrow the book to read.

McKuen doesn't enjoy a particularly good reputation among literary critics, who dismiss him as a pop culture poet and worse. For someone from the unwashed public, however, reading his work gave me a different perspective on writing. He didn't seem to follow any rules, his lines were like sparse sentences, broken up at points to give it a poetical structure. He wrote about simple things, like what he did and didn't do as a child, to more complex emotional issues like losing loved ones, and regret over paths not followed in life, and in doing so, opened for me a world I had never before experienced.

The words spoke to me as no others had done before, and it wasn't long before I was emulating McKuen's style in my own writing. I graduated from sappy rhyming couplets, to excessively earnest free verse, sprinkled with occasional flashes of brilliance. Out of all the poems I wrote in high school and early college, the main period in which I expressed myself in this manner, I'd guess only twenty or thirty are worthy of publication but writing them confirmed for me that this was something I wanted to pursue in life.

I once saw an artist being confronted by someone in the media about why a particular work was considered art, and his response was, "Because I'm an artist and I say it's art." Writing in general, and poetry in particular, conform to a similar standard. Writers write; it's as simple as that. What we say may mean nothing to anyone other than ourselves, but the need to put words on paper cannot be denied.

For every word I've written or published, there are probably thousands of other words of mine which never made it beyond the hand-written or typed rough draft stages. Still, I felt compelled to write them. I find it much easier to express myself in written form than any other. When email and text messaging came about, I found them to be perfect outlets for communicating, and discovering the Internet and Usenet in the 90s, revived my interest in writing, giving me both a forum, and vehicle for publishing ideas quickly.

It has been a long time since I've read *Listen to the Warm*. I don't know that I'd have the same reaction to it now that I did when I was younger but discovering it when I did made me rethink what, to me, constituted writing. Reading the work taught me I needed to define for myself what it means to be a writer. Admittedly, I've had other influences in between, and I've read other works by McKuen that didn't have the same impact, but that one book opened my mind in a way it had never been opened before. The rules went right out the window. *Listen to the Warm* was just what I needed to read at that particular point in my life. I cannot say I wouldn't be a writer if I had not read it then, but I would not be the writer that I am, for better or worse.

Free Bird!

In the annals of fan favorite music, nothing quite compares to the sounds and fans of southern rock as practiced by such luminaries as The Allman Brothers Band, Charlie Daniels, The Outlaws, Molly Hatchet, and the late, lamented, early-70s incarnation of Lynyrd Skynyrd. The genre calls up images of stoic guys, wearing sleeveless T-shirts, driving muscle cars adorned with Confederate flags, with barefoot girls in tight cut-off jeans and halter tops, dancing by the lake, puffing on a J, and knocking back a few PBRs while listening to .38 Special's "Hold on Loosely". The themes of freedom, travel, and uninhibited sex, predominate. Many are set "on the road" and celebrate the vagabond lifestyle, in all its glory.

Frank Zappa once stated that most relationships in the U.S. are screwed up because people get their notions of romance from 50s pop ballads. A lot of negative images of southerners are tied to southern rock from the 70s and 80s. Many southern rock lyrics feature some guy telling his girlfriend he has commitment issues, while in the process of running out on her. Examples include Mr. Breeze, by J.J. Cale, Rambling Man by Dickie Betts, and Take the Highway, by Marshall Tucker.

The stereotypical image of a fan is a guy who got married right out of high school. He now sells auto parts somewhere, all the while wishing he'd started a band, back when the ladies still found him attractive. At home, he retreats to the man cave, downs a few Bud Lites, puts on the LP of The Allman Brothers Live from Fillmore East, and rocks out on air-guitar to "Statesboro Blues".

The main problem with southern rock anthems is that they lend themselves to having their titles shouted out by drunk people at music venues, whether the artist responsible for them is playing or not. It is said that fans of the Allman Brothers once did this with "Whippin' Post" but the best-known example is Lynyrd Skynyrd's "Free Bird". The first documented instance of this was during the encore at Skynyrd's concert at the Fox Theatre in Atlanta in 1977, prompted by a question from lead singer Ronnie Van Zant, and captured for posterity on the album *One More From the Road*. Exactly when the first person yelled it at a concert in which Skynyrd wasn't appearing will never be known, but at one point in history, it was impossible to attend any musical event without someone shouting it out at least once. I heard someone yell it at an Indigo Girls concert at the Beacon Theater in New York around 1990.

In the immediate aftermath of the tragic plane crash, which claimed the lives of Van Zant, Steve and Cassie Gaines, and other members of the crew, some may have done it in tribute to the band, but over time, it just became the thing to yell during a concert. Everyone has done it, though fewer and fewer people realize exactly why anyone does. People born after the late-70s, who may not even know the song, yell it out, probably because they remember their parents and older siblings doing it.

Let's be clear on this: unless one is giving away Charlie Parker albums, the only time it's ever appropriate to yell "Free Bird!" at a concert is when some representative of the Van Zant family asks what song one wants to hear. Any other time, it just annoys the hell out of everyone in the room, and signals to one's date that she'll most likely need to call Uber. There was a time, midway through the phenomenon, when one could get away with it, if it was being done ironically, like at a symphony concert or Dixieland Jazz show, but even these instances wore out their welcome decades ago. Just don't do it.

Trust me, the musicians onstage have heard it from live audiences thousands of times, and don't want to hear it again. They don't find it clever, or amusing. No one does. For those who feel the need to yell something stupid at a show, try something innovative, like "Grooveline" or "Ride of the Valkyries". No one would see that coming.

When Josie Comes Home

We don't know who she is. We don't know where she is, or why. We don't know when, or if she's coming back, and we don't really know how the narrator truly feels about her. Thus, the enduring mystery of Josie, the title character of the final track of Steely Dan's iconic album Aja. The album, which was composed as they returned to their native New York from the West Coast, is all about coming home, and returning to the familiar. How appropriate, then, that it ends with a song foretelling of the return of a mysterious heroine. Initially, it seems, her return will be a joyous occasion, but as is often the case with Steely Dan songs, a nagging sense of disquiet lurks beneath the surface.

The first verse speaks of her acclaim. "She's the pride of the neighborhood," we're told, and the song, at this point, has definite messianic overtones. "She prays like a Roman with her eyes on fire." The lyrics speak of celebrations, rallying in the street, completely overturning the established order. The lyrics imply she may have returned before for brief interludes, but the good times will really commence when she comes home to stay.

Other than this, we're given few details about Josie, other than the implication that she's the spark that will lift her companions from whatever sordid state they've been in. "The raw flame, the live wire." One cannot tell if she's been away of her own free will or not, but it is strongly suggested that the neighborhood hasn't been the same without her. Then, in a telling divergence from the published lyrics, the Dans give us yet another clue to ponder. While the lyric sheet states, "She's the best friend we ever had," on the album, Fagen clearly sings, "She's the best friend we never had." This implies the person telling the story may not even know Josie — that she's now the stuff of legend, and it gives her return an ironic sense of foreboding.

The song contains one of the most recognizable guitar riffs in music. At their show in Alpharetta in 2009, Becker segued into it from an improvised jam, and as soon as he hit the first cord, everyone knew what was coming. Here, again, Donald Fagen replaced "ever" with "never" though on live recordings, which may or may not have featured Fagen singing lead, I've heard it done as written. The music moves with a driving quality, which enhances the imagery of motor scooters, vandalism, and sexual impropriety. Once Josie returns, complacency will be a thing of the past. We're going to take to the streets. Hosanna in the highest! She'll lead us into a whole new era.

Aja is a strong contender for the greatest album ever record-ed. Containing only seven songs, it proves that less is definitely more, and Josie is a fitting end, leaving the listener wondering what could possibly follow it. As it turned out, the follow-up would be the eclectic Gaucho, leading to a maddeningly long hiatus, broken only by the occasional solo album by Fagen or Becker.

Still, Aja was the culmination of everything that had come before, pushing the boundaries of what could be accomplished when all the pieces fell into place. I can think of only a few oth-er bands who could reach such heights. Steely Dan created the perfect musical experience.

When Josie comes home, so good.

Streetcar

A Streetcar Named Desire is heralded as one of the greatest theatrical works of the twentieth century and is one of the best known and most performed works by Tennessee Williams. It sets up a classic confrontation, the flamboyant yet fragile Blanche DuBois versus the menacing and unpredictable Stanley Kowalski. The tension begins the moment Blanche enters the household and builds to its shattering climax with Blanche and Stanley's final confrontation.

The moment Blanche meets her brother-in-law, his fuse is lit, and the question becomes how long it will be before Stanley explodes. Caught between them is the hapless Stella, who tries her best to mediate between two very demanding antagonists without much success. The play also features a decisive shift in power as the first half largely belongs to Blanche, and the second part is clearly dominated by Stanley.

At its heart, Streetcar is a thinly veiled metaphor for the Civil War and Reconstruction. The generation of Southern writers who included Tennessee Williams, Margaret Mitchell and William Faulkner were the children and grandchildren of Confederate veterans, and no doubt grew up hearing horror stories of Northern aggression and the noble Southern gentry who made a valiant but ultimately doomed stand in the face of it. Stanley is the perfect stand-in for the unrefined, egalitarian North with its melting pot willing to assimilate just about anyone, while Blanche represents the genteel and pure-bred South, which existed more in myth than actuality. Everything about Blanche is phony, as was the myth of gallant Southern heroes whose fortunes were, in reality, built on the backs of the slaves and poor whites they exploited.

It speaks to Williams' skill as a playwright that neither character emerges as the hero of the piece. Blanche is portrayed as delusional and elitist, while Stanley is brutish and violent. Stella comes across as the tortured heroine, caught between the empty myth of the "old South" and the harsh reality of the modern industrial North now in control of the South's destiny. That the play takes place in New Orleans, perhaps the most eclectic of old Southern cities, merely enhances the dichotomy of the two extremes.

In many respects, Stella and Blanche are two sides of the same coin, the only difference being that Stella has made compromises Blanche is unwilling or incapable of making. Stella seems the more realistic of the two sisters, seeing the future as grim but manageable with the right attitude, whereas Blanche is unwilling to accept anything but her version of reality. Ironically, it's Blanche who has been treated to the harshest dose of real life, early on losing her husband to suicide, then having to care for the aging members of her family while watching the family's fortunes evaporate due to mismanagement.

Blanche's delusions are rooted in the naive hope that a protector will arise to return her to the gentility she remembers from her youth, whereas Stella's delusions are rooted in her acceptance of the notion that her fortunes are bound to those of her husband. Everything will be fine as long as she does what Stanley tells her. Until Blanche shows up calling into question the relationship Stella has with Stanley, it never occurs to Stella that anything's wrong with her marriage. Blanche is the one to see how controlling Stanley can be and perhaps Blanche's greatest frustration comes from being unable to convince Stella how oppressive this relationship may become.

The challenge of Streetcar is that there's no one within the context of the story that the audience can champion. Blanche is self-centered and delusional, while Stanley is a narcissist, already showing signs of becoming an abusive spouse. Stella simply floats between the two, not knowing for certain which of the powerful presences she should placate. With the exception of Mitch, none of Stanley's friends rise above the level of caricature, and the women surrounding Stella do little more than encourage her to stick by her violent and aggressive spouse.

Stella transforms Stanley into her rugged protector, just as Blanche attempts to transform Mitch into the type of gallant Southern gentleman she thinks will save her. Neither is successful, but at least Stella is able to convince herself that Stanley's failings are more a result of his situation rather than genuine character flaws. The reality is, Stanley needs Stella, and Stella needs Stanley, regardless of how unhealthy their symbiotic relationship may be in the long-run. Stella realizes, though, that as long as she remains within the boundaries set for her by her husband, things will work out for her. Blanche is determined to push those boundaries, much to her detriment.

In most productions, Stanley rarely comes across as likable. While he does have humorous moments, there's a strong sense that the audience is laughing at his oafish ways rather than with him. The turning point comes when he strikes Stella. This is both the point at which Blanche is shown the dark side of Stella's relationship with Stanley, and when the audience realizes how out of control Stanley can become when his authority is challenged. Obviously, we're not seeing Stanley at his best, and Blanche certainly brings out the worst in him, but the violence is there to be mined. He doesn't suddenly turn into an arrogant jerk just because his sister-in-law pays a visit. Stella mentions that Stanley does not give her a regular allowance and generally handles all the bills, both classic traits of a spouse who contrives to make his partner totally dependent upon him.

It's clear from his first appearance in the play that Stanley is firmly in charge in his household. Stella does not seem to mind, instead relinquishing all her autonomy. Like Blanche, she wants someone strong on whom she can depend to support her and make all the decisions, and Stanley is all too willing to fulfill this role. It's entirely likely that their life together has been reasonably pleasant before Blanche shows up with the first real challenge to Stanley, and he doesn't handle it well. Whether or not Blanche's reemergence in Stella's life will have any long-term impact is unknown, but given how she reacts to having Blanche around, it's likely that Stella is ultimately glad her sister leaves at the end, regardless of how that comes about.

Much discussion has centered on Stanley and Blanche's final showdown near the end of the play, and in many productions, it's strongly implied, if not outright depicted that he rapes her. This seems largely dependent upon how the director and cast choose to interpret the scene, though whether or not Stanley actually forces himself on Blanche, it's fairly clear that she does not submit to him out of a sense of mutual desire. By this point in the play, most of Blanche's delusions have been shattered, and one could argue that Mitch's rejection of her has as much, if not more impact on her mental state than anything Stanley does. The balance of power has shifted, and the last safe harbor Blanche was counting on, being with her sister, has not provided her with the solace she needed. Surrendering to Stanley is the final indignity, and a case could be made that Blanche has already gone off the deep end by this point, so nothing Stanley does can have much more of a detrimental effect on her. Blanche has been stripped of all her pretensions, destroying the illusion which was the basis of her self-image. She submits because she has nothing left to lose.

It is important to note, however, that even though Blanche seems defeated at the end, she does not appear to have completely abandoned the delusions she's used to bolster her self-esteem throughout, just as the South itself held onto the notion that it would once again return to its former, imagined splendor. Her final line, "I have always depended upon the kindness of strangers" sounds suspiciously like she believes the person to whom it's said is genuinely doing her a favor. One can imagine Blanche convincing herself that the convalescent home where she's being taken is some sort of elegant chalet arranged for her by a mysterious benefactor, and once she's had time to rest and recuperate, she may well be able to fool the staff into thinking she's safe to release, allowing her to once again return to the belief that she's in control. The Kowalskis probably haven't heard the last of Blanche DuBois.

Kurt Vonnegut and Romanticism

The problem with rapid advances in society and technology is that often we're so concerned with answering the question "Can we?" that we forget to ask, "Should we?" This question is much more difficult to answer, and in the rush to develop the next big breakthrough, people raising legitimate concerns are often drowned out in the discussion of how far we can push the limit. Still these concerns deserve to be heard. By modifying crops to make them more resistant to pests, do we run the risk of making them inedible to humans and animals? Mechanization can free us from labor, but what happens to the legion of workers who previously performed those activities? These aren't easy questions to answer, but if we are to deal with the consequences wrought by technology in modern society, they must be addressed.

Is it any wonder that so many people feel alienated by the modern world? The rise of fundamentalism, the rejection of science and technology, the nostalgia for simpler times and less complex ways of living, are all reactions to the increasingly complex world in which we find ourselves. None of this is new, however, as people have been dealing with questions such as these throughout recorded history. It's no surprise that most of the great art movements of the past few centuries have followed rapid changes in the established social order.

Dadaism sprang up as a reaction to World War I and its shocking level of brutality, and the aftermath of World War II in the U.S. gave us such authors as Joseph Heller, Thomas Pynchon, and J. D. Salinger, while artists such as Andy Warhol and Roy Lichtenstein employed pop culture motifs inspired by the growth of mass media and commercialism in the late 20th century. Art comments on the world around it, and when life becomes increasingly complex, it's the job of artists to try to make some sense of it all. This is probably why absurdist writers such as Beckett, Pinter, and Camus flourished as the world was gripped by the uncertainties of the Cold War, and fears of nuclear annihilation. In a crazy world, sometimes nonsense makes more sense than rationality.

Romanticism arose during the early days of the Industrial Revolution and frequently lamented the potential of industrialized society to rob us of our individuality and humanity. Frankenstein; or, The Modern Prometheus, by Mary Shelly (1818), was a perfect expression of this — humanity reborn without a soul. The creature was a modern vision of humankind, stitched together from many sources and reanimated through unnatural means. It represented the final evolution, humans as creator gods, and raised frightening questions for its author and all who read it. Can one wield the power of a god without the wisdom of a god? It's ironic how often technological innovation is driven by the need to kill, conquer, and subjugate, only discovering non-lethal applications as an afterthought. Splitting the atom first led to weapons of warfare, then to electric power plants.

Science fiction is an outgrowth of Romanticism, and as such is often skeptical about social and technological advances. Nowhere is this better expressed than in the works of Kurt Vonnegut in novels such as Breakfast of Champions, Cat's Cradle, and Slapstick. Vonnegut witnessed, first hand, the destructive side of human nature in all its technological infamy, by being front and center at the Allied bombing of Dresden in February of 1945, the event which inspired what is perhaps his best-known work, Slaughterhouse-Five. In it, Billy Pilgrim becomes a metaphor for post-World War II America, hurtling toward a confusing future, longing for the simplicity of earlier times, and slowly losing his grip on what constitutes reality. "Listen. Billy Pilgrim has come unstuck in time." The Tralfamadorians, the aliens Billy encounters, who see time all at once, in a clear, unchangeable present, speak of the futility of free will. Events are inevitable, and nothing can change them or stop them from happening.

Vonnegut rarely described himself as a science fiction writer, though he acknowledged that people regarded him as such. Rather, he used the conventions of science fiction to tell his story, which any good writer of science or conventional fiction might do. A number of his stories, such as Mother Night and Deadeye Dick, aren't heavily reliant on science fiction, at all, but depict characters famous or infamous for what they've done or are perceived to have done. At heart, Vonnegut shares a kinship with the Romantics in his cynicism for modern humans and the direction evolution seems to be taking us. He tended to blame our "big brains" for most human foibles, and the eventual loss of this biological innovation by humanity in his novel Galapagos, is the salvation of humankind, as the species reverts back to being just another equal player in the natural cycle of predator and prey on earth.

In Player Piano, Vonnegut's first novel, the lead characters destroy the dominant technology, only to see their followers rebuild the most vapid remnants of it to amuse themselves. Vonnegut seems to believe humans can learn from history, but refuse to do so, and it's this refusal that contributes to their worst tendencies. Technology itself is never the villain in Vonnegut's world, except in how humans use it to further their own selfish ends. The culprit for Vonnegut is the belief by humans that they're far cleverer than they actually are, believing they've become masters of the world, when in fact their intervention in the ways of nature often makes things much worse.

Despite his crusty cynicism, Vonnegut nevertheless remained hopeful that humanity could overcome its worst tendencies and somehow live up to its better nature. In his essays, he often cited those he identified as "angels" who were working to combat a host of societal ills such as racism and poverty. An avowed Atheist, he nonetheless admired the lessons of the Sermon on the Mount, and frequently counseled people to show kindness toward one another, reassuring them "you are not alone." In novels such as Slapstick and Cat's Cradle, he tackled the existential problem of living among many, yet still feeling alone and alienated. His principal characters are almost always struggling against the absurdities of human interactions, constantly being victimized by those of lesser mind who are carrying out their own agendas for less than noble purposes. Organized religion was often a favorite target, as was the human tendency to create heroes out of the thinnest of provocations, only to tear them down when the situation changed.

It's no surprise that in many of Vonnegut's novels, the world or the established social order is destroyed and those left are forced to start over with something new, but not necessarily better. Vonnegut seems to view this as the natural progression of life. The old world passes away and is replaced by another, equally confounding one. Through it all, though, Vonnegut refuses to give up hope and encourages us to do the same. In an ever-shrinking world where events on the other side of the globe have the immediacy of what's happening outside our front doors, and many dissonant viewpoints compete for our attention, Kurt Vonnegut still has a voice which rises above the din, guiding us toward a better way of seeing the world and our place in it. It's worth our time to listen.

Myths and Myth Making in Hamlet

Laurence Olivier once referred to Hamlet as the story of a man who can't make up his mind. While there are elements of indecisiveness in Hamlet's actions, to say he can't make up his mind is a gross over-simplification of his situation. Hamlet knows what must be done but doesn't know if he has the moral fortitude to carry out what needs to happen. Hamlet serves as a redemptive figure in the play, lamenting the "heavy-headed revel" the country has fallen into, and from the end of his encounter with his father's ghost, Hamlet realizes that to redeem his country, he may have to pay the ultimate price, losing his life in the bargain. "The time is out of joint: O cursed spite, that ever I was born to set it right!" These are issues he tackles in his most famous speech, "To be or not to be."

Contrary to modern interpretations, the "To be or not to be" soliloquy is not about suicide, but about sacrificing oneself for the greater good. While his "O that this too too solid flesh" speech does touch on the issue of "self-slaughter", Hamlet realizes that if he's to confront the king over the accusations the ghost has made, he'll be putting himself in harm's way. Even if he manages to slay Claudius, he may not have justification enough to save his own life afterward. Regicide, the murder of a king, was both a serious accusation to level against another, as well as a difficult crime to defend against. Ghosts of dead kings make lousy witnesses in court, and there may not be enough remaining evidence for Hamlet to challenge the elected ruler, particularly since he stands to gain the throne himself, making his intentions suspect. By whatever means Claudius gained the throne, he made enough of a case before his peers to justify becoming king over his nephew, who may have been viewed as too thoughtful and not decisive enough to rule with the increasing tensions brought about by Old Hamlet's death.

The play is a balancing act between Hamlet and Claudius. Initially, Claudius puts on a good show of being in charge, dispatching ambassadors to Norway, granting leave for Laertes to return to France, and attempting to get to the bottom of Hamlet's discontent. He appears to be a man at the height of his powers, and at this point, the momentum definitely rests with him. As the first part of the play unfolds, Hamlet slowly balances the scales up to the point he springs The Mousetrap. At that point, the scale temporarily tips in his favor, leaving Claudius to scramble to regain the upper hand. Hamlet knows the truth about his uncle, and whether or not Claudius is fully aware that Hamlet knows of the murder, he at least knows Hamlet is a real enough threat that needs to be eliminated. It's at this point where we finally begin to see cracks in the elaborate facade Claudius has built around himself. He acknowledges, at least to himself in private, that he's guilty of the murder of Old Hamlet, and regrets not being conciliatory enough to purge himself of the crime through his prayers.

The playwright frames the story using the tale of Old Hamlet versus Old Fortinbras thirty years earlier, as related by Horatio in the first scene of the play. Provoked by Old Fortinbras, Old Hamlet defeated him in single combat, thereby securing his kingdom, all of which happened on the day Hamlet was born, as we learn in the scene with the gravediggers. Now, with Old Hamlet dead, and Hamlet not the successor, the throne is no longer secured, and recent actions by Fortinbras make it seem he's preparing to test his claim to the kingdom. Thus we have the "warlike" preparations with which we begin the play, as Claudius, anxious to secure his rule, prepares for a threatened attack. Throughout, Horatio serves as a sort of silent observer and narrator, filling in crucial plot points, and being the one entrusted by Hamlet at the end to convey the story.

The framing device of Fortinbras is often left out of modern adaptations, primarily due to time constraints, and I believe the play loses something in doing so. As written, it provides us with another level of complexity in which to interpret the story and lends weight to the ghost's claim that he must walk the earth, "Until the foul crimes done in my days of nature are burnt and purged away" and suggests an ulterior motive for Old Hamlet's demand for revenge. It provides the play with the outer circle of Old Hamlet killing Old Fortinbras in single combat, followed by Claudius killing Old Hamlet and usurping his kingdom, then Hamlet killing Polonius, provoking Laertes's revenge against Hamlet which leads to Laertes's death as well, and finally, Hamlet killing Claudius before dying himself. Hamlet's only act as king is to name Fortinbras as his successor, thereby restoring to Fortinbras the kingdom Old Hamlet took from his father and bringing the story full-circle.

One reason Hamlet may resonate with audiences is because its basic story echoes some of the oldest mythic traditions in humankind, in particular those of the fertility gods such as Attis and Adonis. Hamlet serves as just this sort of redeeming figure, the sacrificial king who, by his death, purges his land of its corruption. This is a theme as old as civilization itself, as early agrarian societies lived by the ebb and flow of the seasons, growth in the summer, harvest in the fall, death in the winter, rebirth in the spring. Myths of dying saviors such as Attis feature the same sort of sacrifice, the blood of the dying king rejuvenating the soil, making it fertile again. Early succession rituals celebrated the dead king reborn in the person of the son. It's no surprise that Hamlet is said to be thirty years old, the same age Jesus is reported to be in the Gospels, as both serve a similarly redemptive role in his respective story.

The main source for Shakespeare's Hamlet appears to have been Gesta Danorum, a collection of myths and histories set in Denmark and written by Saxo Grammaticus in the 12th century. Shakespeare most likely used the French translation by Francois Belleforest, which came out in 1570 and is said to have more direct parallels to Shakespeare's story. The story told by Shakespeare was further altered to fit into the conventions of an Elizabethan revenge tragedy. The parallels between Saxo Grammaticus's story and Shakespeare's include the murder of an eavesdropping courtier, and a visit to England meant to dispose of the prince. In the original Danish story, Amleth, as he's known, makes it to England, raises an army and successfully opposes his uncle for the throne. Saxo's Amleth is fully a man of action, though he, too, feigns madness to avoid detection by his uncle.

The story of a usurped king and avenging son, with a murdering uncle and fickle queen, seems to also echo the myths surrounding Agamemnon, Clytemnestra, and Orestes, which are, themselves, echoes of the Egyptian myths of Osiris, Isis, and Horus. Orestes, the avenging son in this tale, is a descendant of the cursed House of Atreus, which arose from the grandsons of Tantalus. Part of the story of Agamemnon parallels that of Jephthah in Judges 11:34-39, which Hamlet alludes to while talking to Polonius about Ophelia.

In some versions of the myth, Agamemnon is murdered by his wife, Clytemnestra, in part for the sacrifice of his daughter Iphigenia at the start of the Trojan War. Clytemnestra also has an affair with Agamemnon's adopted brother Aegisthus, who takes part in the murder. In the stories surrounding Orestes, he takes revenge by killing both his mother and his uncle and in some dramatizations, Orestes is driven mad by his actions, which finds it's parallel in Hamlet's feigned madness in both Saxo's and Shakespeare's work. Whereas the god Apollo instructs Orestes to kill Clytemnestra, with Hamlet, the ghost explicitly tells him the opposite in regard to his mother, "Leave her to heaven."

The play we know as Hamlet seems to have been revised from an infamous earlier attempt by Shakespeare or another playwright, which had met with considerable derision from critics of his time. The existing play makes a number of references to this earlier attempt throughout, in particular while Hamlet is instructing the actors, though there are other subtle references to it elsewhere in the script.

From the references in Shakespeare's play, we can surmise it must have been badly over-written and over-acted. "The croaking raven doth bellow for revenge," Hamlet says during the play within a play, which sounds like something a critic would write, and may have been lifted from an actual review of the original work. Other scenes feature lines which also seem to be recalling an earlier failed attempt, such as when Hamlet tells the players:

> "...O, it
> offends me to the soul to hear a robustious
> periwig-pated fellow tear a passion to tatters, to
> very rags, to split the ears of the groundlings, who
> for the most part are capable of nothing but
> inexplicable dumbshows and noise: I would have such
> a fellow whipped for o'erdoing Termagant; it
> out-herods Herod: pray you, avoid it."

The language again suggests the words of a critic and may have been taken verbatim from what people were saying about the original.

After dispatching Rosencrantz and Guildenstern to England with Hamlet, Claudius makes a speech in which, on the surface, he seems to be asking England to rid him of his problematic nephew. One can imagine, however, the playwright standing before the audience speaking the lines, asking them to kill the memory of the previous play:

> "...thou mayst not coldly set
> Our sovereign process; which imports at full,
> By letters conjuring to that effect,
> The present death of Hamlet. Do it, England;
> For like the hectic in my blood he rages,
> And thou must cure me..."

If Hamlet does originate with an earlier attempt by Shake-speare, the parallels to Greek mythology place the original closer to the time Titus Andronicus was written, as it, too, contains passages which reference the myths surrounding the House of Atreus. In particular, the manner in which Atreus takes revenge on his brother Thyestes finds itself recreated in how Titus avenges himself against Tamora and Saturninus. Niobe, the aunt of Atreus and Thyestes, who's turned to stone and weeps continuously over the loss of her children as punishment for insulting Demeter, is mentioned by Hamlet in his "too too solid flesh" soliloquy at the beginning of the play.

At the conclusion of Orestes' story, he atones for the sins of his family and lifts the curse from the House of Atreus. Hamlet is not so lucky, as evidenced by one of his last speeches where he implores Horatio to tell his story:

"...what a wounded name,
Things standing thus unknown, shall live behind me!"

Despite Hamlet's redemptive function within the play, Shake-speare does not make it part of Hamlet's destiny to reign as king himself. To this end, the murder of Polonius, Hamlet's one impulsive act within the play, serves its function, sullying Hamlet, and garnering the vengeance of Laertes. In the end, though, Hamlet completes his mission, and in his sole act as king, by conveying the election lights on Fortinbras, he turns the kingdom over to someone who can restore order to the land. The dying king takes upon himself the sins of his people, thereby clearing the slate and allowing them to start anew. The cycle of death and renewal continues on.

The Tragedy of Juliet

Shakespeare's best-known tragedy is the story of two star-crossed teenagers, who, in death, end their families' conflict. Despite being hailed as a great romance, Romeo and Juliet is not a love story, but very much about individual responsibility and the consequences of making decisions in the heat of passion. Romeo is very impulsive in his actions, never thinking about the harm he may be causing and bringing about much needless strife for himself and those around him. Juliet emerges as a tragic figure, unwittingly caught up in the increasingly violent tensions between the families, in which Romeo is a willing participant.

I refer to the play as the comedy of Romeo and the tragedy of Juliet. Most who've studied the play note that the first half has the wistful feel of one of Shakespeare's comedies, with the lovelorn Romeo first pining away for Rosaline, then quickly forgetting her when he spies Juliet at the Capulets' party. The light-hearted tone is cast aside with the death of Mercutio at Tybalt's hands, which leads Romeo to avenge Mercutio's death by taking Tybalt's life. From that point on, the play becomes darkly tragic as the focus shifts from Romeo to Juliet.

The play is laced with violence, both actual and implied. Other commentators have pointed out that the play presents numerous examples of what has come to be known as "toxic masculinity". Notably, the fight between Mercutio and Tybalt which leads to first Mercutio's then Tybalt's death, is one such example. There's also a lot of subtle violence in how the characters interact with one another. In the scene where Juliet balks at marrying Paris, Lord Capulet's reaction shows exactly how daughters were regarded in history. Capulet states that she's his property, and he may dispose of her as he chooses, a sentiment echoed in other works by Shakespeare, including the beginning of the comedy A Midsummer Night's Dream.

We see a demonstration of Capulet's temper early in the play, when ordering Tybalt not to take action after finding Romeo has crashed the Capulets' party. At first, Capulet seems reasonable, lauding the favorable reports he's heard of Romeo's behavior, but as Tybalt presses the issue, he provokes the anger of Lord Capulet, who quickly abandons his festive appearance to let his kinsman know who's in charge. The hot-headed Tybalt can't let the issue drop, though, leading to his confrontation with Romeo, which Mercutio takes up on Romeo's behalf when Romeo tries to walk away.

Every bad thing that happens in the play happens as a consequence of something Romeo does and at each turn, he has alternatives he never takes the time to consider. He pines over Rosaline, so his friends take him to the Capulets' feast, where he meets Juliet, then immediately forgets Rosaline. He woos Juliet, and hastily marries her, without considering the consequences of secretly marrying into the family of his family's sworn enemy. When confronted by Tybalt, he chooses to say nothing of his union to Juliet, first allowing the situation to escalate between Tybalt and Mercutio, then coming between them, which allows Tybalt to deliver the fatal wound. Up to this point in the play, Romeo hasn't done anything, other than hastily marry Juliet, to cause him any lasting problems. He soon changes all that, setting in motion the series of events which leads the play to its devastating finale.

After killing Tybalt, Romeo runs away, declaring, "I am fortune's fool!" In reality, fortune had nothing to do with it, as Romeo had many options which did not include fighting Tybalt. When Romeo is first provoked and chooses to walk away, his best option was to do nothing, and just let Mercutio handle it, since, as a kinsman of the Duke, Mercutio is in a better position to deal with the fall out. Once Tybalt kills Mercutio, Romeo again needs to do nothing. Following the Duke's decree, when Mercutio falls, Tybalt has signed his own death warrant. Romeo would best be served to walk away and let Tybalt face his punishment. Even if his family connections are enough to save him from death, Tybalt would, at the very least, be banished, which would also solve Romeo's problems without getting his hands dirty. Once again Romeo acts impulsively, this time costing Tybalt his life, and Romeo his freedom of movement within Verona and his actions have devastating consequences for the woman he claims to love.

Romeo's irresponsible actions leave Juliet in a terrible position, first having to reconcile her love for Romeo against her devotion to her cousin Tybalt, then, finding herself offered as a bride to Paris, which puts her at odds with her short-tempered father. Her nurse counsels Juliet to simply yield to the will of her father and marry Paris, but Juliet knows that it's not that simple. While it's not explicitly spelled out in the context of the play, the reality is that once Juliet has spent the night with Romeo, she's no longer a virgin. Capulet has been promising Paris the hand of his virginal daughter and once the older and worldlier Paris has sex with her, he's likely to suspect she's not and, if so, will undoubtedly raise the issue with Capulet. Judging by his response to her reluctance to marry Paris, there is little doubt how Capulet would respond to the embarrassment such a revelation would cause him. Juliet's only real hope is for Romeo to return and claim her hand, and given his situation, that's not likely to happen. Under these circumstances, suicide or cloister are her only viable options and she has Romeo to thank for that.

There is a definite pattern to Romeo's behavior which calls into question how much he truly cares for Juliet despite all his flowery language. This is evident from the beginning of the play, when it's revealed that the Rosaline Romeo claims to love is Capulet's niece. This suggests that Romeo's trouble with Rosaline isn't that she's rejected him but that she is off-limits to him because of her family connections. He's pining for her because the situation between their families makes it impossible for him to pursue her. In this context, his motives must come under scrutiny, since all accounts are that he's as much an active participant in his family's feud with the Capulets as are the rest of his kinsmen. Lady Montague expresses relief that Romeo was not party to the fight which starts off the play. Why then would Romeo choose a relative of the Capulets as the object of his affection, knowing fully well that it would only lead to more conflict?

Meeting Juliet at the party and learning of her parentage presents Romeo with a new opportunity to needle his family's sworn enemy. He immediately puts his life at risk to pursue it by sneaking back onto the grounds of the Capulets' home that night to see Juliet. Romeo shows his true colors when he allows Tybalt to goad him into a fight once Mercutio is dead. Not even his professed love for Juliet, Tybalt's cousin, is enough to prevent him from striking out at his enemy when provoked.

Every production I've seen has cast actresses playing Juliet who are in their late-teens to mid-twenties. However, the text makes it clear that Juliet is thirteen. Lord Capulet questions whether Juliet is old enough to marry when the subject of her betrothal to Paris first comes up in the play. We're not specifically told Romeo's age, but given his companions, it's safe to assume that he, Benvolio, Mercutio, and Tybalt are close in age, late-teens to early-twenties at the oldest. Paris is a count, that is, landed gentry, meaning he is "of age" or no younger than twenty-one to twenty-five and possibly as old as thirty.

The life expectancy of people in this era was early- to mid-forties, and under English common law, boys of fourteen and girls as young as twelve could act as witnesses to wills and executors of estates. While men tended to forestall marriage until they had some means of subsistence, usually a plot of land on their families' property or the guarantee of a substantial inheritance, women could be betrothed as soon as they reached sexual maturity so long as their families were in agreement. Given the hazards of childbirth, women tended to die younger, and it wasn't out of the ordinary for men to marry several times, leading to very young women being wedded to much older men, particularly if there were young children in the man's household who needed care.

While we may find it scandalous that a man in his twenties or thirties is pressing for a marriage to a thirteen-year-old girl, as Paris does in the play, in that day and age, it was fairly commonplace. For one thing, it got the woman out of her father's house and made her the responsibility of someone else. Daughters in this era weren't held in very high esteem and were generally prized more for the powerful men they could attract than for their own personal attributes.

Juliet is the only character in the play who does not have an overt agenda. The Capulets and Montagues are consumed with their feud, which may or may not influence Romeo's decision to pursue women related to his family's enemy. Paris wants Juliet as his wife and Capulet wants the prestige that comes with joining his daughter to a kinsman of the Duke. Friar Laurence is largely motivated by his desire to end the bloodshed caused by the feud, agreeing to sanction a union which he should know neither side will accept. Juliet's nurse at first helps Juliet in her pursuit of Romeo but shows her reliance on the established order when she counsels Juliet to marry Paris when Romeo is sent away. Juliet finds herself caught between her obedience to her father and her love for her father's enemy yet remains focused on what she believes to be the right course of action, remaining faithful to the vow she made to Romeo. In doing so, she becomes the only character who consistently grows throughout the play.

Romeo becomes more reckless and impulsive as the action progresses, whereas Juliet becomes more mature and assured of her actions. Romeo's decision to kill himself after hearing erroneous reports of Juliet's death is yet another rash and foolish act which could have been avoided, if only he had checked in with Friar Laurence when he arrived back in Verona. Juliet, on the other hand, looks for any opportunity to rectify the situation without further bloodshed. When she realizes her family views her as little more than a token to be offered to the influential Paris, she resolves to chart her own course, even if it means ending her life, and while she is fully prepared to die rather than violate her vow to Romeo, she allows Friar Laurence to counsel her and gratefully accepts his remedy for her situation.

Once again, she falls victim to Romeo's impulsiveness. Seeing her last chance at happiness on her own terms taken from her, she exercises the only option she feels she has left and ends her life. As is the case with many of Shakespeare's tragic heroines, fate has ruled against her, but rather than remain its pawn, she renders her own judgment, and dies with the man she loves.

The Madness of Ophelia

Modern stage interpretations of Hamlet place a great deal of emphasis on the relationship between Hamlet and Ophelia, more so, perhaps, than the playwright intended. Some go so far as to place the pair in the same category as other great tragic couplings, Romeo and Juliet, Antony and Cleopatra, and Othello and Desdemona, to name a few. Many cite Hamlet's rejection of Ophelia, his murder of Polonius, and his exile to England as the leading causes of Ophelia's madness in the play. While these are important factors in Ophelia's breakdown, there's a more definitive cause that has been overlooked by most who comment on it, though it is spelled out quite plainly within the text of the play. Equally so, evidence suggests Shakespeare never intended for these characters to be paired, at least not in the same way other couples in the dramas and comedies have been portrayed.

Judging by Shakespeare's other works, if there was any sort of relationship intended between Hamlet and Ophelia, Shakespeare would have gotten to the point more quickly and left no doubt as to how they related to each other. With other famous couples, their affection or antagonism toward one another is established fairly quickly in the play, onstage and in full view of the audience. Beatrice and Benedick from the comedy Much Ado About Nothing, encounter one another in the first scene of the first act. Romeo and Juliet, perhaps Shakespeare's most tragic couple, meet very early in the play and interact extensively onstage after meeting.

Hamlet and Ophelia, by contrast, only have two direct onstage encounters and the first is engineered by Polonius and Claudius, not the characters themselves. While Hamlet's first encounter with Ophelia starts out playfully, it turns hostile once he realizes they're being spied upon. Hamlet sits with her at the play within a play, but their conversation does not imply an intimate relationship between them, despite the number of crude jokes Hamlet makes at Ophelia's expense.

The play makes it clear from the start that Hamlet has been away at school in Wittenberg and only returned to Elsinore because of his father's death, and by all accounts, he's not taking it well; nor is he happy with his mother's decision to marry Claudius, or Claudius taking the throne instead of Hamlet. Given all that's weighing on his mind, why would Hamlet suddenly start writing love letters to Ophelia? Her words on the topic imply that this is something that's ongoing, though we're never told when she first started receiving these missives. Admittedly, it's implied that a lot of time passes in the play, or at least that the time has been compressed, but Polonius's warning to Ophelia follows immediately after her farewell to Laertes, which comes directly after the scene at court where we've seen Hamlet as an emotional wreck and not the amorous suitor described by Ophelia.

While Ophelia speaks of Hamlet's attentions toward her, we see no direct evidence of it onstage, with the exception of Hamlet's behavior at her grave — and the grave scene has numerous other inconsistencies to it. In fact, most of the appearances of Ophelia in the play can be removed without harming the flow of the narrative, which suggests her involvement came from a different play, or from a very different version of the play than the one we know. She doesn't have a speaking part during the initial scene where Claudius is holding court at the start of the play and plays little role in the play within a play scene where Hamlet exposes Claudius's guilt in Old Hamlet's death. Hamlet's murder of Polonius is enough to spur Laertes's need for revenge without adding Ophelia's madness to the mix.

Ophelia's description of Hamlet's behavior when he comes to her chambers makes his actions sound very odd, but the only onstage source we have for this account is Ophelia herself. In the chronology of the play as it exists in adaptations following the First Folio, the scene Ophelia describes falls just after Hamlet has encountered the ghost, learned that his uncle most likely killed the King and usurped the kingdom, and sworn his friends to secrecy about it. It seems highly unlikely that after being told in very dramatic fashion to avenge his father's murder, that Hamlet's first thought would be to drop in on Ophelia to pursue what's been described as a meaningless dalliance.

Another problem skewing the narrative seems to be that the scenes, as presented in the First Folio, are out of sequence. In the so-called "Bad Quarto" believed by some to have been a scaled down version of the play for traveling productions, the first direct encounter between Ophelia and Hamlet, the scene where he implores her to cloister herself (Get thee to a nunnery), occurs before Hamlet's scene with her father, where Hamlet compares him to a fish monger. In the First Folio and all subsequent editions, it occurs afterward. One clue is in the "To be or not to be" soliloquy, that precedes Hamlet's first encounter with Ophelia.

This speech more logically follows Hamlet's encounter with the ghost, as it does in the "Bad Quarto" rather than a spontaneous musing later in the play as in most modern adaptations.

In his first encounter with Ophelia, when she tries to return his letters and trinkets, Hamlet acts like he doesn't know what she's talking about and denies giving them to her. After Ophelia insists Hamlet did give her the letters, he begins to suspect she's being deceitful and questions her honesty; then he speaks of the incompatibility between beauty and honesty. It's during this exchange where Hamlet says "I did love you once" but this statement cannot be taken as evidence of romantic intent on Hamlet's part, since the word "love" appears to have multiple connotations in Shakespeare's work.

Elsewhere in the play, when Hamlet is short with Rosencrantz, he replies, "My lord, you once did love me" and a moment or so later, Guildenstern says, "if my duty be too bold, my love is too unmannerly" which confuses Hamlet. In these instances, "love" seems to be equivalent to "respect" or "concern" and, taking the context from the admonishing tone Hamlet assumes later in his initial scene with Ophelia, one way to interpret "I did love you once" would be "I once respected you." Ophelia's response plays on the more common meaning of the word, causing Hamlet to correct her, "I loved you not". He then berates her for her vanity and implores her to go to a nunnery, asking "Why wouldst thou be a breeder of sinners?"

Throughout history, and particularly in Shakespeare's time, a woman in the lower gentry who became pregnant by a noble was often hastily married off to someone of her proper station to cover it up, and this would have been well-known to Shakespeare's audience. One such example was Emelia Bassano, who became pregnant while she was the consort of the Lord Chamberlain, Henry Carey, and was married off to Alphonso Lanier. Hamlet's meaning in telling Ophelia to cloister herself is made clear in his next utterance, after realizing they're being spied upon, "If thou dost marry... be you as chaste as ice, as pure as snow..."

This idea is made more explicit in Hamlet's conversation with Polonius, where Hamlet calls him a fishmonger. After asking Polonius if he has a daughter, Hamlet counsels Polonius:

> "Let her not walk i' the sun: conception is a
> blessing: but not as your daughter may conceive."

Polonius misses the significance of the speech, believing it to be a lovelorn rant, but these instances mark two notable times in the play where Hamlet expresses concern over Ophelia's chastity. His use of the word "sun" in his conversation with Polonius is significant in helping to sort out what Hamlet means. In his first appearance in the play, Hamlet utilizes a pun on the word "sun" to indicate the king. "Not so my lord, I am too much i' the sun." In careful terms, Hamlet is warning Polonius to not let his daughter catch the attention of Claudius.

Before the players enter, Hamlet refers to Polonius as Jephthah, the biblical judge of Israel, who sacrificed his daughter in fulfillment of a promise to God in exchange for victory over the Ammonites (Judges 11:34-39). The story of Jephthah has many points in common with the ancient Greek legends about Agamemnon, who sacrificed his daughter Iphigenia for favorable winds to sail to Troy. Aeschylus's play about Agamemnon and his son, Orestes, seems to have been derived from the same myths and legends that influenced the Danish tales upon which Shakespeare based Hamlet. From this, it appears Hamlet is warning Polonius that he's unwittingly sacrificing his daughter in exchange for favor at court.

More importantly, Ophelia's description of Hamlet's actions when he comes to her chambers sounds completely at odds with the brooding and melancholy prince Shakespeare has presented up to this point, who so far has done little more onstage than lament his father's death and his mother's marriage and react to seeing his father's ghost. When Polonius tells Claudius and Gertrude of Hamlet's attentions toward Ophelia, Gertrude is skeptical that this is the actual cause of Hamlet's distress, though she acknowledges it as a possibility. The two times we witness Hamlet with Ophelia, he either keeps her at arm's length or taunts her for supposed sexual improprieties. Any attentions he shows her are mainly for the benefit of others in the room, who already suspect him of admiring Ophelia, and seem designed to reinforce their belief in his odd behavior. He does seem to imply she's either in a relationship with or being pursued by someone, just not him.

A better candidate for who's been showering Ophelia with attention is Claudius. He's already committed murder to gain the throne and win the hand of Gertrude, his sister-in-law, which was considered an incestuous act as implied within the play, so adultery and assault certainly wouldn't be a problem for him. While most will point out that Ophelia specifically says it's

Hamlet, and has a letter signed by him, this doesn't mean Claudius isn't the actual culprit. When he returns from his aborted trip to England, Hamlet tells Horatio that he has his father's signet ring, identical to the one Claudius uses, which Hamlet used to seal the order condemning Rosencrantz and Guildenstern to death. It's not until Hamlet receives the letters from Ophelia that he questions her honesty. Hamlet would have seen the seal and may have realized where the letters originated, even if Ophelia wasn't sure.

One question to ask is whether or not Hamlet is the given name of the character and his father, or the family name, since both father and son bear that name. We have a parallel instance with old and young Fortinbras. It was common in Shakespeare's time for nobles to be known by their title or family names rather than their given names, which would have been taken for granted by Shakespeare's audience, and "Claudius" could either be the throne name Hamlet's uncle adopted to distinguish himself from his brother, or his given name. If this is true, then Claudius could also be known as Hamlet, since he's the brother of the king and the uncle of the prince by that name. Numerous clues within the context of the play support the idea that Claudius and not Hamlet has his eyes on Ophelia.

Before Ophelia enters in her mad state, Gertrude refuses to see her. Horatio insists that Gertrude talk to her, claiming Ophelia's rantings have set off scandalous rumors throughout the kingdom. While we're not told specifically what Ophelia has been saying, in the brief interlude before Ophelia enters, Gertrude alludes to it:

"To my sick soul, as sin's true nature is,
Each toy seems prologue to some great amiss:
So full of artless jealousy is guilt,
It spills itself in fearing to be spilt."

When Ophelia enters, her opening line is dripping with sarcasm toward the king, "Where is the beauteous majesty of Denmark?" After Gertrude speaks to her, she immediately launches into a song for Gertrude:

"How should I your true love know
From another one?
By his cockle hat and staff,
And his sandal shoon."

From there her lyrics begin to allude to her father's death, invoking images of a headstone, shrouds, and a grave. Once Claudius enters and addresses her, however, all Ophelia's songs change their tone and theme, switching from a lost loved one, to a lost lover, and are directed at Claudius, prompting him to make several attempts to plead with her. Her most explicit song is:

> "To-morrow is Saint Valentine's day,
> All in the morning betime,
> And I a maid at your window,
> To be your Valentine.
> Then up he rose, and donn'd his clothes,
> And dupp'd the chamber-door;
> Let in the maid, that out a maid
> Never departed more."

Why is Ophelia singing about the loss of her chastity simply because her father died? There's been no suggestion of an incestuous relationship between them, and while Polonius did not always act warmly toward her, his treatment of her was not outside the bounds of a typical father and daughter relationship as depicted elsewhere in Shakespeare. Also, there's no suggestion that she and Hamlet had a sexual relationship, though Polonius, and possibly Laertes, suspected it was possible.

After Claudius pleads further with her, she concludes:

> "Quoth she, before you tumbled me,
> You promised me to wed.
> So would I ha' done, by yonder sun,
> An thou hadst not come to my bed."

Ophelia's use of "sun" is telling here, since Hamlet has already established it as a metaphor for Claudius.

Once Ophelia leaves, Claudius is quick to relate what she's said to grief over her father, but, as Polonius said, "Though this be madness, yet there is method in't." Ophelia's behavior is that of someone who's suffering from severe psychological trauma. Her father's death must surely have been traumatic for her, particularly with the implied cover up of what happened, but Ophelia's brother was still alive and would need to return to handle his father's affairs, and she probably had every reason to expect she'd be able to count on the support of others at court to help her deal with the loss. So, while it was traumatic, Polonius' death in and of itself is probably not what pushed Ophelia over the edge. Her behavior, combined with the lyrics of the songs she directs at Claudius, strongly implies she's been sexually assaulted, and she also makes it very clear who she's accusing.

Throughout Shakespeare's work, young women are often the target of nefarious rogues looking to take advantage of them, and a king is at liberty to do just that, since someone making accusations against a king is at a severe disadvantage. We see this very situation in Measure for Measure, where the Duke uses his power and privilege to attempt to force the virtuous Isabella, into a sexual liaison. Young, unmarried women are often referred to in Shakespeare as property of their fathers or families, since they did not have the legal capacity to consent on their own.

When Polonius confronts Ophelia about Hamlet early in the play, his concern is mostly for how badly it reflects on him than on Ophelia, and a number of her mad songs allude to losing her virginity outside of a marriage which would have required her father or family's consent. Since much of the action in Hamlet happens offstage, we can surmise that it would be completely in character for Ophelia to turn to the King for comfort and answers about her father's death, just as it would be totally in character for Claudius to take advantage of her already fragile state. Loss of her father followed by the loss of her innocence is more than enough to bring about the mental state she exhibits in her mad scenes.

Polonius implies that rumors are circulating of Ophelia entertaining Hamlet in private, but Ophelia does not confirm this, other than in the one scene where she describes Hamlet's behavior in her chambers, and she implies this is unwelcome attention on her part. From her discussion with Polonius early in the play, it sounds like most of the entreaties from Hamlet have been in writing, or through trinkets delivered by messengers. When he presents his case to Claudius and Gertrude, he reads a letter signed by Hamlet, but does not present evidence of face to face encounters between Hamlet and Ophelia.

Seducing women in disguise was a favorite tactic of Henry VIII, which is highlighted in Shakespeare's play about the monarch. In other plays, such as Loves Labors Lost and The Taming of the Shrew, major characters disguise themselves to pursue love interests. Such behavior by Claudius could have been a relic of the play that didn't survive the rewrites or was excised when the play was compiled for publication or, perhaps, the audience took this for granted since it was a favorite device used by the playwright. It's possible Ophelia knows who's been wooing her, but because it's the king, she's purposely vague in relaying the info to her father, who misunderstands what she's trying to tell him. This wouldn't be out of the ordinary, given that this is the chief dynamic of Polonius. The first scene with Ophelia and Laertes seems to suggest otherwise, however, since Laertes clearly alludes to the prince, and Ophelia does not correct him. However, sometimes in Shakespeare's work, kings are referred to as princes.

This casts a new light on Ophelia's death, which also happens offstage. The only account we have comes from Gertrude and it's not clear whether she's speaking as an eye-witness or was relating what someone told her. According to her account, Ophelia fell into a brook while trying to retrieve some flowers and didn't have the presence of mind to save herself before her soaked clothing pulled her under the water. Given how vivid her description is, it's implied that Gertrude witnessed the drowning, which begs the question of why no one on shore attempted to save Ophelia. If Gertrude was present, she no doubt had the typical entourage a Queen would have surrounding her, so it seems someone should have been able to get to Ophelia before she went under. Gertrude makes no mention of any rescue attempts, other than stating that Ophelia didn't try to save herself.

People who make accusations against a king, even in a distracted state, don't last very long. Gertrude's reluctance to deal with her earlier suggests she had a motive to silence Ophelia as well. At the graveside, the priest expresses doubts that Ophelia's death was accidental as was claimed, though he suggests she killed herself. His suspicions imply that Gertrude's account was not accepted as the undisputed truth.

At the graveside, according to the Folio, Gertrude says she had hoped Ophelia would be Hamlet's wife, which seems curious given how much emphasis was placed early in the play by both Polonius and Laertes on telling Ophelia that she could not pursue a relationship with Hamlet due to his royal status. Gertrude was also part of the discussion Polonius had with Claudius regarding Hamlet's attentions toward Ophelia where Polonius revealed he told Ophelia Hamlet was "out of thy star" and she expresses doubts that Ophelia is the cause of Hamlet's melancholy. In the First Quarto, Gertrude expresses regret that her flowers won't adorn Ophelia's marriage bed, not that she would marry Hamlet, which seems a more likely sentiment given the circumstances.

Hamlet's behavior at the grave is curious as well. In his outburst over Ophelia's death, Hamlet doesn't seem to recall that he killed Laertes's father, which was a factor in the mental state that may have contributed to the death of Laertes's sister, and can't understand why Laertes might have a problem with him popping up at Ophelia's funeral to profess his love for her. Also, after spending much of the first half of the play keeping Ophelia at arm's length, and, at one point, outwardly accusing her of using her beauty to drive men mad, Hamlet suddenly decides she's the love of his life, to the extent that he's willing to make a spectacle of himself at her funeral, again uncharacteristic of the prince we've come to know. Right afterward, Hamlet exhibits guilt over his treatment of Laertes, but once again seems to forget how much in love he was with Ophelia, as she's never again mentioned by him.

If we remove the entire graveside scene from the play, the flow of the narrative goes from Horatio meeting with the sailors to the scene where Hamlet explains his return from England to Horatio, just before receiving Laertes's challenge. None of the interplay between Hamlet and the gravediggers furthers the narrative, except for adding the information that Hamlet is thirty years old, which would have been middle-aged in Shakespeare's time.

In the very next scene after the funeral, Hamlet tells Horatio how he learned of Rosencrantz and Guildenstern's betrayal and how he thwarted them, which one presumes he should have already told Horatio since they were talking just prior to the graveside scene. Just as Hamlet's attentions to Ophelia don't make much sense in the context of his situation at the start of the play, the discussion between Hamlet and Horatio about Alexander and death don't fit the context of Hamlet suddenly reemerging in Denmark when he's supposed to be in England. The only purpose of the scene at the grave seems to be to give closure to Hamlet and Ophelia's relationship, which the play has not promoted in the first place.

Hamlet has always been regarded as an enigmatic play and confusion over the relationship of Ophelia and Hamlet only contributes to that reputation. Generations of theatrical troupes have invested much time wringing every bit of subtext from a relationship that simply is not supported by the narrative of the play. We have three surviving contemporary editions with significant variations between them. These contribute to the ambiguity of Ophelia and Hamlet's relationship which allows actors and directors to reinvent the nature of it for each new generation. For all that happens to her, the reality is that Ophelia is largely known by the reactions she invokes in other characters than for her own direct effect on the action of the play. She remains the archetypal loving sister and obedient daughter broken by the tragedies of her life, which is a tragedy in and of itself.